THE COMING *SPIRITUAL EARTHQUAKE*

Another Perspective of the Coming Raptures

James T. Harman

Prophecy
Countdown
Publications

THE COMING *SPIRITUAL EARTHQUAKE*

Copyright © 2021, James T. Harman

Prophecy Countdown Publications, LLC
P.O. Box 941612
Maitland, FL 32794
www.ProphecyCountdown.com

ISBN: 978-0-9636984-5-2

All references from Scripture are from the New International Version (NIV) copyright © 1973 unless noted from the following translations:
> KJ – King James Version
> ESV – English Standard Version®, copyright © 2001 Crossway
> NLT – New Living Translation, copyright © 1996
> NKJV- New King James Version, copyright © 1982
>   by Thomas Nelson, Inc. Used by permission.

Words in bold emphasis are authors and not in original Scripture.

Numerical references to selected words in the text of Scripture are from James H. Strong Dictionaries of the Hebrew and Greek words.

Certain words such as Kingdom and Judgement Seat are capitalized to emphasize their importance, but not in accordance with Traditional fashion.

Credit and Copyright for pictures inside this book:
> Page 16 – Bride with veil (#504) courtesy of: www.EricaKoesler.com
> Page 84 – *The Bride* by Dorothy Luscombe

After reading *The Coming Spiritual Earthquake*, it answered so many questions that other traditional teachings were lacking in key areas. Now, the book of Revelation makes more sense. Jim Harman has a gift, which allows him to use scripture to support doctrine as he lets the Bible interpret itself. His book will renew your desire to be the overcomer God wants us to be.

Donald B. Driskell – Madison, MS

Jim Harman's new book is important because it helps to explain where most of today's popular prophecy books have serious errors in interpretation that will deceive many. I believe that when the First Fruit Rapture takes place so few believers will be taken that most people will not even know they are gone, which is completely different from what is taught today.

Lyndon Navarre – Port St. Lucie, FL

I read Jim Harman's book *The Coming Spiritual Earthquake*. For reasons stated in my books I do not find the partial-rapture position persuasive. In any event, let us suppose, for the sake of argument, that the partial rapture position is correct. In that case, many unfaithful believers will be given a second chance to qualify for inheriting the kingdom if they are left behind. So, for the sake of the unfaithful, let us hope that Jim is right so that they can have a second chance. In my view, however, they are given no second chance. Accordingly, some full-rapture misthologists have correctly deduced that when unfaithful believers stand before the Bema, they will wish that they had been left behind to go through the tribulation. Carnal believers will wish that it had been a partial rapture.

Marty A. Cauley
Author of *The Outer Darkness*
www.misthology.org

The message presented in *The Coming Spiritual Earthquake* is greatly needed to awaken believers to the false assumptions many have when it comes to the Rapture. I might have titled it: *The Rapture Earthquake*.

Ray Brubraker
God's News Behind the News

In Matthew 24:3-8 the disciples asked Jesus when shall these things be and what shall be the sign of your coming and of the end of the world?...and there shall be famines, and pestilences [Covid 19]... Thank you so much for being obedient to God and writing your book *The Coming Spiritual Earthquake* to help prepare people for the times we are living in. It would be awesome if everyone read it now while there is still time. Jesus is coming very soon! *"Even so, come, Lord Jesus."* (Rev 22:20)

Ima Dean Jones – West Fork, AR

In his book, *The Coming Spiritual Earthquake*, James Harman makes a compelling case for the need for believers to be spiritually ready to meet the Lord. Unfortunately, most Christians are unprepared for such an encounter. Whenever the rapture, I'm certain of one thing: it will resemble much more closely what James lays out in his book than what is typically portrayed in Christian movies. It is imperative that we repent of our love of the world and press into the Lord like never before!

Steve Gallagher – Author of *Standing Firm through the Great Apostasy*

Prologue

The message of this book was born from a horrifying dream I had in which I found myself in the period the Bible describes as the Tribulation.

I seldom dream; however, this dream was so real and terrifying that it motivated me to search the Scriptures to determine who will be able to escape this dreadful time of testing, and how a person can prepare.

I believe the Lord gave me this in order to help people prepare to be *"found worthy to escape"* the Tribulation. It is my prayer it will be used by our loving, heavenly Father to touch the lives of those He wants to reach with this urgent message.

In His Love,

Jim Harman

Dedication

This book is dedicated to all Overcoming,
First Fruit believers, looking for the
soon return of our loving Lord and Savior,
Jesus Christ.

Table of Contents

It is important to point out that the doctrine of a "partial" or "phased" Rapture of believers was actually taught by our Lord on two separate occasions. The reader is encouraged to see Chapter 5 of *Overcomers' Guide To The Kingdom* that can be downloaded on our website: www.ProphecyCountdown.com

This teaching was revived during the Philadelphian Church era around the turn of the 20th century by such men as Govett, Patton, Lang, and A.B. Simpson. For an interesting study on this "partial" or "phased" Rapture, please see: *Oil In Your Vessel* by A.B. Simpson (founder of the Christian Missionary Alliance). This article can also be found on the above website.

Dr. Ray Brubaker, who wrote the following Foreword was one of the last great proponents of this important teaching. Ray founded *God's News Behind the News* back in 1944, and boldly proclaimed Christ's soon return and the need to be ready. While he went to be with the Lord a few years ago, his many followers from around the world will not forget how he would sign off each of his newscasts:

> *Therefore be ye also ready: for in such an hour as ye think not the Son of man cometh.* (Matthew 24:44 (KJ))

Foreword

I'm convinced no message is more exciting than the message of our Lord's Return for His Own. It is the Blessed Hope of the believer in Christ. It is the message of this book.

However, when prophecy scholars lose sight of this message and get caught up in, and devote more time to the New Age Movement or the New World Order, than to our Lord's Coming, there should be great concern.

And, there is great concern for those who believe their profession of faith in Christ is all that is needed to prepare one for the Rapture when the Lord comes for His Own. While coming to know Christ as Savior is absolutely important, there are many admonitions given to believers to "watch" and "be ready" for our Lord's Coming.

Surely revival must come to the heart of the person living in known disobedience to the will of God upon realizing their carelessness and indifference. This condition, which constitutes "lukewarmness," could result in their lack of being ready when our Lord returns.

If looking for our Lord's Return, will we not want to be ready for that glorious event?

As we read in I John 3:2-3:

> ... when He shall appear, we shall be like Him; for we shall see Him as He is. And every man that hath this hope in Him, purify himself, even as He is pure.

The message presented in *THE COMING SPIRITUAL EARTHQUAKE* is greatly needed to awaken believers to the false assumptions many have when it comes to the Rapture.

This book will be used by the Holy Spirit to awaken you to the nearness of our Lord's Return, along with preparing you: to the need of living daily for Christ; to be ready when He comes.

May God grant it. Amen.

Ray Brubaker
God's News Behind the News
December 1992

Preface

One of the biggest false ideas in the church today is that all Christians will be going in the Rapture when Jesus Christ snatches His bride up to the throne.

One of the second biggest false ideas is that no one knows when it is going to be. By not properly interpreting the Word of God, these misconceptions have greatly contributed to the lukewarm condition of the church today. Jesus Christ foresaw this current state and warned the present church in Revelation 3:16:

So then because thou art lukewarm, and neither cold nor hot, I will spew thee out of my mouth.

There is coming a great **SPIRITUAL EARTHQUAKE** that will shake the Church. Many will wake-up to find they are part of the multitude of believers living in the Tribulation period.

This book is a final warning to the Church:

REPENT, THE KINGDOM OF HEAVEN IS AT HAND.

May God use this message to awaken many in our churches in order to prepare to meet the Bridegroom.

It is time for the wise virgins to trim their lamps and be ready to enter into the marriage chamber (Matthew 25).

Only those who have **kept** His word and who are found **looking** for Him will be counted worthy to escape the coming tribulation. All others will be tried in the time of testing to be ushered in by the *COMING SPIRITUAL EARTHQUAKE*.

1996 International Prophecy Conference

Ray Brubaker's annual prophecy conference was one of the most popular gathering places for people to hear the top Bible teachers from around the world.

In 1996, the conference was held in Tampa, Florida and included over a dozen of the leading prophecy teachers including:

- Jack Van Impe
- J.R. Church
- Grant Jeffrey
- Perry Stone
- David Breese
- Peter Lalonde
- Tim Lahaye

Having written the Foreword to this book, Ray Brubaker also felt led by the Lord to invite Jim Harman to present its important message.

Jim's 30 minute presentation which is entitled: *The Bride Has Made Herself Ready* can be viewed under the Bride Tab on his website at: www.ProphecyCountdown.com

Introduction

———————————⟡———————————

Debate has gone on for years as to whether Jesus would return before the Tribulation period (pre-trib), in the middle of it (mid-trib) or at its end (post-trib).

This confusion has fostered an attitude that prophecy is too difficult to understand for the average Christian. As a result, the real truth in the Word of God has remained hidden from the believer.

Critical Time

The Church is at a very critical point. Jesus is getting ready to remove His First Fruit believers from this planet, to be followed by the horrible Tribulation period.

Revelation 7:9-17, warns of a **great multitude** which no man could number, coming out of the great Tribulation period. It will be shown that these represent many in our churches today for whom martyrdom will be required as described in Revelation 12:11.

Time To Prepare

Prior to the Rapture, all Christians are given the opportunity of preparing for that event. Those who are Overcomers, counted worthy to escape the tribulation period, will be caught up to the throne of God, while all others will be required to be Overcomers by not shrinking from death.

It is time for the Church to **wake up** and **repent** before it is too late. The coming *SPIRITUAL EARTHQUAKE* will be far more devastating than any economic earthquake or shaking of the earth's surface!

Timing of Events

In an attempt to determine when the Lord is going to return, many dates have been set and many have been disappointed when those dates have come and gone.

Because of this, popular tradition has emerged that it is wrong to discuss its timing, and that we are not supposed to know when the Lord is going to return.

This presents a problem since we are rapidly approaching the **COMING SPIRITUAL EARTHQUAKE**, and many believers will be taken by surprise. The day is almost upon us, and Paul warned us in I Thessalonians 5:4:

> *But you, brothers, are not in darkness so that this day **should** surprise you like a thief.*

Paul is telling us that Christians should not be surprised. By implication, Paul was saying that some Christians will indeed be surprised, even though they should not be taken by surprise. Hosea 4:6 warns us:

> *My people are destroyed for lack of knowledge: because thou hast rejected knowledge, I will also reject thee...*

Christians need to return to the Holy Word of God to see what it says about knowing when the Lord is going to return. Instead of listening to church tradition, this book will help the believer better understand what God's word has to say about the timing of end time events that are about to culminate in the **COMING SPIRITUAL EARTHQUAKE**.

Readers need to approach this material with an open mind, teachable spirit and heart of love. We all need to be like the Berean Christians who searched the Scriptures daily to be sure what even the Apostle Paul told them was the truth (please see Acts 17:11).

If believers fail to properly divide the word of Truth (II Timothy 2:15), they will be misguided and may find themselves in the horror of the Tribulation period. Jesus warned us of this in Matthew 23:13-14:

> *Woe to you, teachers of the law and Pharisees, you hypocrites! You shut the kingdom of heaven in men's faces. You yourselves do not enter, nor will you let those enter who are trying to.*

Jesus was admonishing the Church leaders! The very ones that should know the Truth are actually keeping others from finding the correct way!

One of the main purposes of this book is to help guide people back to what the Word of God actually says and to help them prepare to meet the Bridegroom.

ARE YOU READY TO MEET JESUS WHEN HE RETURNS FOR HIS BRIDE?

...that He might present her to Himself a glorious church, not having spot or wrinkle or any such thing, but that she should be holy and without blemish.
(Ephesians 5:27 – NKJV)

The Spirit and the bride say, Come...
(Revelation 22:17)

Chapter 1 – Wise Will Understand

As the Church approaches the end of the sixth millennium from creation, it would be wise to listen to the words of Apostle Paul's companion and fellow-preacher Barnabas:

> And even in the beginning of the creation he makes mention of the Sabbath. And God made in the SIX DAYS the works of his hands; and he finished them on the seventh day, and rested the seventh day, and sanctified it.
>
> Consider, my children, what that signifies, he finished them in six days. The meaning of it is this; that in SIX THOUSAND YEARS the Lord God will bring all things to AN END.
>
> For with him ONE DAY is a THOUSAND YEARS; as himself testifieth, saying, Behold this day shall be as a thousand years. Therefore, children, in SIX DAYS, that is, in SIX THOUSAND YEARS shall all things be accomplished. (Barnabas 13:3-5)

This sounds strikingly similar to what the Apostle Peter had to say when discussing the end times:

> *But DO NOT FORGET this one thing, dear friends: WITH THE LORD A DAY IS LIKE A THOUSAND YEARS, and A THOUSAND YEARS ARE LIKE A DAY...* (II Peter 3:8)

Both Barnabas and Peter were telling us how God measures time. A day in His time frame is the equivalent to 1,000 years in the life of man. Since He created the earth in 6 days and then rested on the seventh, He was giving mankind a prophecy of how long He was going to deal with the human race on this earth.

At the end of 6 days or 6,000 years, His Word will be finished and mankind will then move into the 1,000 years of rest described in the book of Revelation.

There were approximately 4,000 years from creation until Christ, giving us 2,000 years since His first coming, for a total of 6,000 years. (Appendix D is provided to show the reader another possible sign regarding this 2,000 year time frame).

6,000 Years Almost Up?

Colin Deal's article *The Last Trumpet Decade*, which is available on our website under the **Supplemental Articles** for this book, believes that Jesus was anointed as the Messiah between 26 to 29 AD, and this anointing of Christ occurred precisely 4,000 years after the creation of Adam! He shows that, "If we add 2,000 years to 26 / 29 AD we arrive at 2026-2029 AD! This means that 6,000 years from Adam's creation should be completed sometime during this decade!"

Since Jesus left this earth about 2,000 years ago, He has only been gone about 2 days in His time frame. With this understanding, Hosea's prophecy brings on added importance:

> *After TWO DAYS he will revive us; on the THIRD DAY he will restore us, that we may live in his presence.* (Hosea 6:2)

This is a prophecy that after two days, or 2,000 years, God will restore us to live in His presence. After the second day we will dwell with the Lord in the coming Millennium (His third day). This time relationship is also spoken of by our Lord in several instances. One example is found in John 2:1: *"On the THIRD DAY a wedding took place..."* This was a prophecy that after the end of the second day, or on the third day the Wedding described in Revelation 19:7, will take place. 2,000 years after the first coming of Christ, the bride will rejoice in her Wedding to the Lamb at the start of the 1,000 year millennium reign. The Word of God is a rich and wonderful store-house for those who are diligently seeking His truth. God has a master plan for mankind that is rapidly winding to a close.

Religious Spirit

Whenever a date for the Lord's return is discussed, the first objection that most people make is, "You can't know the day or the hour, therefore let's not even discuss it." The argument goes on to say that it is wrong to discuss dates and that no one knows when Jesus is going to return.

Let's be careful that we are not like the Pharisees and Sadducees who were rebuked by Jesus himself in Matthew 16:2-3(KJ):

> When it is evening ye say, "It will be fair weather; for the sky is red." And in the morning, "It will be foul weather today: for the sky is red and lowring." O YE HYPOCRITES, ye can discern the face of the sky; but can ye not discern the SIGNS OF THE TIMES?

The religious leaders at the time of Christ were rebuked because they could not discern the time that they were living in. Scholars have shown that had they read the Scripture with a proper heart, they would have known the time they were living in and they would have known to be looking for their Messiah. In a similar manner, we are currently living at a time when the Scriptures are shouting: **JESUS IS COMING!**

Unfortunately, not everyone has the "ears to hear" or the "eyes to see" what is transpiring before them.

Because of the tradition that we can not know about the timing of end-time events, many people will be caught off guard at the *COMING SPIRITUAL EARTHQUAKE.*

Day And Hour

To ensure that we are not rebuked by Jesus, let's take a better look at what the Word of God has to say about knowing the timing. The most widely used verse people quote when they want to prove that we are not to know when Jesus is returning is found in Matthew:

> But of that day and hour knoweth no man, no, not the angels of heaven, but my Father only. (Matthew 24:36)

What most people fail to remember, however, is the preceding verse:

> Heaven and earth shall **pass away**, but my words shall not pass away. (Matthew 24:35)

The day and hour that no one knew about when Jesus spoke those words was when heaven and earth will pass away at the end of the 1,000 year Millennium. The timing of when this will occur is found in Revelation 21:1:

> Then I saw a new heaven and a new earth, for the first heaven and the first earth had passed away.

The reason that this time is not known is found in Revelation 20:3, which says Satan is let out of the bottomless pit at the end of 1,000 years for: "a LITTLE SEASON." No one but God knows how long Satan will have to deceive the nations at that time.

Hour You Think Not

The next objection to knowing the timing of end time events is related to the following verses in Matthew 24:42-44(KJ):

WATCH therefore: for YE KNOW NOT WHAT HOUR your Lord doth come. But know this, that if the GOODMAN of the house had known in what WATCH the THIEF would come, he would not have suffered his house to be broken up. Therefore be ye also ready: for in such AN HOUR AS YE THINK NOT the Son of man cometh.

On the surface of things, it appears that the Lord is coming as a thief and at a time we will not know. For the answer to this, we need to turn over to the parallel passage in Luke where Peter asks the Lord a very vital question in Luke 12:39-41(KJ):

And this know, that if the goodman of the house had known what hour the thief would come, he would have watched, and not suffered his house to be broken through. Be ye therefore ready also: for the Son of Man cometh at AN HOUR WHEN YE THINK NOT.
Then Peter said unto him, LORD, SPEAKEST THOU THIS PARABLE UNTO US, OR EVEN TO ALL?

In this parallel passage concerning when the Lord is going to return, Luke records a very important question that Peter asks: Is this parable for US, meaning fellow believers, or for everyone? Before we look at the Lord's answer, let's remember why the Lord spoke in parables:

...Why do you speak to them in parables? He replied, "The knowledge of the secrets of the kingdom of heaven has been given to you, but not to them.
(Matthew 13:10 & 11)

Unto you it is given to know the mystery of the kingdom of God: but unto them that are without, all these things are done in parables: That seeing they may see, and not perceive; and hearing they may hear, and not understand. (Mark 4:11 & 12)

Jesus used parables, because not everyone is given knowledge to the mysteries of the kingdom. Peter's question about who Jesus meant in the parable of not knowing the timing becomes an essential point.

Now, let's see what the Lord's answer is to this crucial question:

> *And the Lord said, Who then is that **faithful** and **wise** steward, whom HIS lord shall make ruler over his household, to give them their portion of meat in due season." "Blessed is <u>that</u> servant, whom his lord when he cometh shall find so doing. Of a truth I say unto you, that he will make him ruler over all that he hath.*
> *But and if that servant say in his **heart,** My lord delayeth his coming; and shall begin to beat the menservants and maidens, and to eat and drink, and to be drunken; The lord of that servant will come in a day when he **looketh not** for him, and at an hour when he is **not aware,** and will cut him in sunder, and will appoint him his portion with the unbelievers.* (Luke 12:42-46)

First of all, Jesus says that the *faithful* and *wise* steward will be greatly blessed. They are dressed and *ready* with their lamps burning brightly *waiting* and *watching* for their Lord to return (see Luke 12:35-36 and Matthew 25:10).

But notice what the *unfaithful* servant is thinking in his heart: *"My lord delayeth his coming."* He is **not** looking and watching as the faithful and wise steward is. Instead, he is beating (Greek: wounding the conscience) of his brothers and sisters. He is saying: *'no one knows'* when the Lord is coming, so 'let's forget about it and talk about something else; let's concern ourselves with this present time and enjoy ourselves.'

Because of the attitude of the unfaithful servant's heart, Jesus says that he comes for him: *"in a day when he **looketh not***

for Him, and at an hour when he is not aware." To the
unfaithful servant Jesus is coming like a thief. He is going to
take him by surprise on a day and hour that he will not expect
Him.

The wise and faithful servant will be ready, waiting and
watching for Jesus, while the unfaithful servant will not know
and will be taken by surprise.

Thief In The Night

This teaching that the wise and faithful will know and the
unfaithful will not know is also confirmed for us by Paul:

> *Now, brothers, about times and dates we do not need to
> write to you, for you know very well that the day of the
> Lord will come like a THIEF in the night. While people
> are saying, "Peace and safety," destruction will come
> on them suddenly, as labor pains on a pregnant woman,
> and they will not escape.*
> (I Thessalonians 5:1-3)

Most people stop reading at the end of the third verse to try to
prove their point that the Lord is going to come as a thief. He is
coming like a thief, but to whom is He coming to as a thief?
Notice what Paul says in the fourth verse:

> *But you, brothers, are not in darkness so that this day
> should surprise you like a THIEF.*

Paul is saying that the Lord's coming should not surprise the
Christian (**brother**).   While the rest of the world will be
surprised like a thief, the Christian should not be surprised.

This confirms what Jesus was teaching us in His parables. The
wise and faithful steward will be READY, WAITING and
WATCHING for Him when He comes for them. The unfaithful

and foolish servant will not be looking for Him and will be taken by surprise.

Looking For Jesus

Further evidence for this teaching is found in the book of Hebrews. Hebrews 10:25 shows that the faithful servant will, *"see the day approaching."* How could we see the day coming if we are not supposed to know? By simple implication, we should know.

Not only should we know, but more importantly we should be looking for Him as taught to us in Hebrews 9:28:

> *So Christ was once offered to bear the sins of many; and unto them **that look for Him** shall he appear the second time without sin unto salvation.*

This makes it quite clear, Jesus is returning the second time for those who are looking for Him. In subsequent chapters we will review what looking for Him entails, and the fate of those who fail to heed God's Word.

Further, the book of Revelation implies the faithful will know when the Lord is coming:

> *I know your deeds; you have a reputation of being alive, but you are dead. **Wakeup!** Strengthen what remains and is about to die...Remember, therefore, what you have received and heard; obey it, and repent. But **if** you **do not wake up**, I will **come like a thief**, and you will **not know** at what time I will come to you. (Rev.3:2-3)*

The church of Sardis was dead. The Lord rebuked it and warned it to repent and to wake up. By implication, if this church will only obey His admonition, they will not be surprised like a thief and they *will know* the time.

The Word of God is very clear. The wise and faithful servant will be looking for Jesus and they will be ready, waiting and watching for Him. They will know the time and will not be taken by surprise.

The unfaithful and foolish servant will not know when Jesus returns and they will not be ready for Him. They will be taken by surprise like a thief and they will not know the day or hour when He will return.

The choice is left up to the individual. He can heed the Word of God and be looking for the soon return of Jesus, or else he can continue listening to the tradition of not knowing and be taken by surprise like a thief.

Know It Is Near

Finally, Jesus commanded us to **know** the timing of end time events:

> *Now learn a parable of the fig tree; When his branch is yet tender, and putteth forth leaves, ye know that summer is nigh: So likewise ye, when ye shall see all these things, **know** that it is near, **even at the doors**..* (Matthew 24:32-33 (KJ))

Just prior to telling us the fig tree parable, Jesus listed all of the signs that we would see, such as: wars and rumors of wars, nation rising against nation, famines and earthquakes in diverse places. These signs were just the beginning of birth pains, indicating that the time for delivery (Tribulation period) was just about due.

Then Jesus gives us one of the most important clues to knowing His return is near. He tells us to LEARN a parable or lesson about the FIG TREE. Most Bible students agree that the Fig

Tree represents the nation of Israel (See Hosea 9:10 and Joel 1:6-7).

Until this century, Israel had been scattered throughout the world with no land to call home. Then on May 14, 1948, the state of Israel was founded and on May 15, 1949, was recognized by the United Nations.

Jesus tells us that once we see the nation of Israel established again we can and **should know** that His return is near, even at the **door**!

When someone knocks on your door or rings the door bell, what do you do? Of course, you get up, and go to the door. Jesus was telling us that once we see all the signs converging on the world scene, AND we see Israel established as a nation, we are to **know** that He is as close as the front door. In other words, it is time to get up, get ready, Jesus is almost here!

Wise Will Understand

The book of Daniel ends with words that are prophetic for the time we now live:

> *Go your way, Daniel, because the words are closed up and sealed until the time of the end. Many will be **purified**, **made spotless** and **refined**, but the wicked will continue to be wicked. None of the wicked will understand, but those who are **wise** will understand.* (Daniel 12:9-10 – NIV)

May Daniel's words reverberate in the reader's ears as they continue in this book. Many will be *purified* and *made spotless* and *refined* and the *wise* will understand.

Chapter 2 – Escape Possible

———————⟨◇⟩———————

Another clear indication we are nearing the return of the Lord, is the fact that the world is crying for peace and safety.

On September 27, 1991, President Bush announced a New Era of "Peace and Security" with sweeping nuclear arms reductions, as he took America off alert from possible attack from Russia.

Since the Middle East peace process began in October of 1991, it has only progressed to the point where the parties **talk** about peace and security. The Apostle Paul warned us of this time:

> *For yourselves know perfectly that the Day of the LORD so cometh as a thief in the night (for the ungodly). For when they shall SAY, **peace and safety**, then sudden destruction cometh upon them, as travail upon a woman with child; and they shall not escape.*
> (I Thessalonians 5:2-3(KJ))

Paul was telling us that there would come a time when the world was **talking** about **peace** and **safety**. He was warning us that **talk** is all it really is. The nations say they want peace, but we know that there will be no true peace until the "Prince of Peace," Jesus Christ returns.

Jeremiah reminds us: "Peace, peace," they say when there is no peace." (Jeremiah 6:14)

The main point needs to be understood that while they are **saying** peace and safety, then sudden destruction will come. At some point, everyone will believe that peace has been achieved. When that point is reached, Watch Out! - for the Bible declares when they are saying peace and safety, then will come *"sudden destruction."*

Day Of The Lord

This sudden destruction will usher in the time described in the Word of God, as the DAY of the LORD. The Day of the Lord is a major doctrine that is referred to more than three hundred times in God's word.

The Day of the Lord begins with the 6th Seal of the Tribulation period, to be followed by the 1,000 years of peace during the reign of Christ. The beginning of the Day of the Lord will be one of most horrible times for the inhabitants of the earth. It will be a time of testing and great trial. Revelation 6:8, indicates that one-quarter of the people will die. And of those remaining, Revelation 9:15, shows one-third of mankind will perish. Taken together, this tells us that one-half of the population of the earth will be destroyed during this awful time.

Shelter Possible

While this coming period of destruction will be horrible for those left on the earth, the Word of God does indicate that there is a way of escape:

> *The great day of the Lord is near, it is near, and hasteth greatly, even the voice of the day of the Lord: the mighty man shall cry there bitterly. That day is a day of wrath, a day of trouble and distress, a day of wasteness and desolation, a day of darkness and gloominess, a day of clouds and thick darkness, a day of trumpet and alarm against the fenced cities, and against the high towers.* (Zephaniah 1:14-15 (KJ))

> *Before the decree bring forth, before the day pass as the chaff, before the fierce anger of the Lord come upon you, before the DAY of the LORD'S anger come upon you.*

> *Seek ye the Lord, all ye meek of the earth, which have wrought his judgment; seek righteousness, seek meekness: it **may be** (or **perhaps**) ye **shall be hid** in the day of the Lord's anger.* (Zephaniah 2:2-3 (KJ))

The prophet Zephaniah indicated that some of those who are seeking the Lord, may be able to be hid from the horrible day of the Lord. He says to seek the Lord, and perhaps you will be able to escape.

Notice that he does not indicate that you are definitely guaranteed of escaping. He uses the words *may be* or *perhaps*, which would mean that not everyone will be able to escape.

Lord's Same Teaching

Jesus confirms this same teaching for us:

> *Watch, ye therefore, and pray always, that ye **may be accounted worthy** to escape all these things that shall come to pass, and to stand before the Son of man.* (Luke 21:36(KJ)

Jesus told us to always pray that we *may be* able to escape. Jesus was telling this to His disciples. He is telling the Christian to pray that he is counted worthy of escaping the Tribulation period. This indicates that escape is possible, but is conditioned upon being accounted worthy in the Lord's eyes.

Both the prophet Zephaniah and the Lord show that escaping the Day of the Lord (or the Tribulation period) is possible. They both indicate that it is conditional and not something that is guaranteed or assured.

Jesus indicated that the Christian needed to pray they may be accounted worthy in order to escape. This infers that not all

Christians are automatically counted worthy. If they were, then Jesus would not have told us to pray such a prayer.

If all Christians were already guaranteed that they would escape the Tribulation period, then this instruction would be meaningless.

It is important to remember that we are not talking about salvation. We are talking about escaping the Tribulation. No one is worthy of salvation. We are saved completely by the grace of God:

> *For by grace are ye saved through faith; and that not of yourselves: it is the gift of God: Not of works, lest any man should boast.* (Ephesians 2:8-9 (KJ))

In the following chapter we will look further into what Jesus meant when He told us to pray that we are **accounted worthy** of escaping the horrible Tribulation period.

Chapter 3 – Counted Worthy To Escape

*Watch, ye therefore, and pray always, that ye **may be accounted worthy** to escape all these things that shall come to pass, and to stand before the Son of man.*
(Luke 21:36(KJ)

Jesus told us that we need to **watch** and **pray** always that we are accounted **worthy** in order to escape the terrible Tribulation period that will soon engulf this world. Escape is very possible, but it is also very conditional. It is not guaranteed or assured for any one. The Word of God makes it very clear that not all Christians are worthy and not all Christians will escape the Tribulation period.

Who Is Worthy?

Revelation 3:4, tells us:

*Thou hast a **few** names even in Sardis which **have not defiled their garments**; and they shall walk with me in white: for they **are worthy**.*

The second and third chapters of Revelation list seven churches which represent Christians. They are all believers in Christ, but only a **few** have the promise of escaping the Tribulation period.

In Revelation 3:4, we see that the Church of Sardis had a **few** members who stood out from the rest. Overall, the Church of Sardis was dead; but it did have a few who were found **worthy**. They were found **worthy** because they had not defiled their garments.

Jesus is returning for His bride. He expects her to be without spot or wrinkle and to be holy and without blemish (Ephesians 5:27).

While the Church of Sardis was dead, it did have a few members who had not defiled their garments. They had kept them spotless without any wrinkle or blemish. Because of this, they were considered **worthy**.

Remember that Jesus told us to pray that we are counted **worthy** to escape the Tribulation period. This picture of the few in Sardis shows us what it takes to be worthy.

Jesus is telling His bride not to get her wedding garment dirty by this dark and dying world. To stay away from anything that would cause her to get her dress wrinkled or spotted. And to keep herself separate from the things of this world and remain Holy and pure.

By so doing the bride of Christ will be ready and found **worthy** when the Lord returns for her. As a result, she will be able to escape the Tribulation hour.

Kept From Tribulation

Revelation also gives us another Church that is given the promise of escaping the horrible Tribulation period:

> *Because thou hast **kept the word** of my patience, I also will **keep thee from the hour of temptation** (Tribulation), which shall come upon the world, to try them that dwell upon the earth.* (Revelation 3:10 (KJ))

This is the Church of Philadelphia. Because the members of this Church have **kept God's word,** God promises to keep them out of the Tribulation period. This is also what James was trying to tell the Church:

> *Do not merely listen to the Word, and so deceive yourselves. **Do what it says**.* (James 1:22)

By keeping God's Word, the Christian is given the promise of escaping the Tribulation hour. By not defiling their garment, the believer is considered worthy. By doing what the Word of God says and not soiling or wrinkling her wedding gown, the bride of Christ can be confident that Jesus will take her to be with Him prior to when the Tribulation hour begins.

Those Not Worthy

The Word of God also describes a group of believers who are not considered worthy:

> *The kingdom of heaven is like a king who prepared a wedding banquet for his son. He sent his servants to those who had been invited to the banquet to tell them to come, but they refused to come.*
>
> *Then he sent some more servants and said, "Tell those who have been invited that I have prepared my dinner...and everything is ready. Come to the wedding banquet.*
>
> *But they* **paid no attention to it** *(KJ:* **made light of it***), and went off--one to his field, another to his business...*
>
> *Then he said to his servants, "The wedding banquet is ready, but those I invited did not deserve to come (KJ: were* **not worthy***).* Matthew 22:2-5, and 22:8

Because they did not pay attention to the invitation to come to the wedding banquet they missed out. The King James version says that they even made light of it. Because of their response, they are considered: **not worthy.**

Earlier we showed that only those who are accounted worthy by the Lord, will be able to escape the Tribulation period. Since this group makes light of the message, they will find themselves in the Tribulation hour.

This is a parable for today's Christian. When the subject of the return of Christ is brought up, many Christians make light of it or pay no attention to it. They are too caught up with the things of this world to be concerned with thoughts of heaven. Because of their attitude, they are **not considered worthy**.

For a parallel passage to the above, the reader may want to study Luke 14:16-24. In Luke's version, everyone makes excuses on why they can not come to the wedding banquet.

They were also caught up in the things of this world; and as a result, they made excuses and ended up missing the banquet. In subsequent chapters we will discover that there are more references that show multitudes of Christians ending up in the Tribulation period. This is so unnecessary, because God does provide a way of escape. Those who are accounted worthy and who have not defiled themselves with this evil world will be kept from the hour of testing that is coming to try this world. Escape is possible for those who are found worthy and looking for Him.

Chapter 4 – Make Every Effort

We have seen that escaping the Tribulation period is not automatic or assured for any Christian. Only those who have "*kept the word*" and who have "*not defiled their garments*" are given the blessed assurance of escaping the Tribulation and being found **worthy**.

This implies that effort is required of the believer in order to escape the hour of trial. While salvation is a free gift that can not be obtained by works (Ephesians 2:8-9), escape from the time of testing is based upon the merits of the individual believer's life.

Made Herself Ready

A good illustration of this is seen in the bride of Christ:

> *Hallelujah! For our Lord God Almighty reigns. Let us rejoice and be glad and give him glory! For the wedding of the Lamb has come, and His **bride has made herself ready.*** (Revelation 19:6-7)

Just as any earthly bride prepares for her wedding day, the bride of Christ has to make preparations for her wedding to the Lamb of God. Effort is required in order to be ready. Further proof of this is seen in the verse which follows:

> *Fine linen, bright and clean, was given her to wear. (Fine linen stands for the righteous **acts** of the saints.)* (Revelation 19:8 – NIV)

This indicates that the righteous acts of the believer is what provided the spotless wedding garment. Effort is required on the part of the believer if they want to have the fine linen that the bride of Christ is wearing.

(The above translation of Revelation 19:8, is from the New International Version (NIV). In this instance, it gives a truer rendering of the original Greek. Some will argue that the fine linen represents the righteousness that is imputed to the believer through Christ. This error helps foster the lukewarm attitude that will lead many Christians into the Tribulation period).

Ten Virgins

For further proof that effort is required, let's look at the parable of the ten virgins:

> *At midnight the cry rang out: "Here's the Bridegroom! Come out to meet him!" Then all the virgins woke up and trimmed their lamps. The foolish ones said to the wise, "Give us some of your oil; our lamps are going out.*
>
> *"No," they replied, "There may not be enough for both us and you. Instead, go to those who sell oil and buy some for yourselves." But while they were on their way to buy the oil, the Bridegroom arrived. The virgins **who were ready** went in with him to the wedding banquet. And the door was shut.* (Matthew 25:6-10)

Here we see that only the five wise virgins who were **ready** went into the wedding. The Greek for ready is: fit, prepared, or made ready.

While it appears the five foolish virgins were very busy, they were not properly prepared or ready when the Bridegroom arrived. This is a picture of the Church today. Many appear to be very busy, but they are not making the proper preparations. They are not busy making themselves ready to meet their Bridegroom. We need to learn a lesson from the five wise virgins and prepare our lives to be ready to meet our Bridegroom: Jesus, when He returns for His bride.

Necessary Preparations

In discussing prophecies concerning the end of time, Peter gives the Christian some very vital instruction:

> *....I have written.....as reminders to stimulate you to wholesome thinking. Since everything will be destroyed in this way, what kind of people ought you to be? You ought to live **holy** and **godly** lives as you look forward to the day of God and speed its coming...So then, dear friends, since you are looking forward to this, **make every effort** to be found **spotless, blameless** and at **peace** with HIM.* (II Peter 3:1,11&14)

Peter tells us we need to **make every effort** to be found **blameless** and to live **holy** and **godly** lives. This is further confirmation that effort is required by the believer. Jesus is coming for the believers who have made the necessary preparations. Those who are found spotless, blameless and at peace with Him will experience great joy at His return.

The Apostle Paul also taught us how we should be living when he was instructing the Church of the Thessalonians about the return of the Lord:

> *You are witnesses, and so is God, of how **holy**, **righteous** and **blameless** we were among you who believed. For you know that we dealt with each of you as a father deals with his own children, encouraging, comforting, and **urging** you to **live lives worthy** of GOD, who calls you into His kingdom and glory.*
> (I Thessalonians 2:10-12)

> *May he strengthen your hearts so that you will be **blameless** and **holy** in the presence of our God and Father when our Lord Jesus comes...*
> (I Thessalonians 3:13)

*Finally, brothers, we instructed you how to live in order to **please** God, as in fact you are living. Now we ask you and URGE you in the Lord Jesus to do this more and more.* (I Thessalonians 4:1)
*For God did not call us to be impure, but to live a **holy life**.* (I Thessalonians 4:7)

Paul's instruction is vital to the Christian. God wants His children holy, pure, righteous and blameless. This type of life is necessary in order to be considered worthy. Paul was concerned that the believers in the Church might not be found worthy. Notice his remarks in his second letter to this church:

*All this is evidence that God's judgement is right, and as a result you will be **counted worthy** of the kingdom of God...* (II Thessalonians 1:5)
*With this in mind, we constantly pray for you, that our God may **count you worthy** of His calling...*
(II Thessalonians 1:11)

Paul knew the believer was not automatically counted worthy before God. He urged them to live their lives in such a way that God might find them properly prepared for the Kingdom of God. He then relates that he constantly prayed for the believer's worthiness! This sounds strikingly similar to the words the Lord told his disciples in Luke 21:36:

*Watch, ye therefore, and pray always, that ye **may be accounted worthy** to escape all these things that shall come to pass, and to stand before the Son of man.*

It becomes abundantly clear that worthiness before the Lord is not a condition that is automatically bestowed upon the believer at the time of salvation. If it were, Jesus and Paul would not have stated prayer was needed to ensure the Christian is found worthy.

Upward Calling

Paul realized that being counted worthy before God was of vital importance. He urged the disciples to live their lives in such a way that they may be found acceptable before God, and he prayed they may achieve this calling.

Remember that Paul was the believer who wrote the following words in Ephesians 2:8-9:

> *For by grace are ye saved through faith; and that not of yourselves: it is the gift of God: Not of works, lest any man should boast.* (Ephesians 2:8-9 (KJ))

Paul knew that works played no part in his salvation. And yet, Paul also wrote the following words, which indicate he was very concerned about his own life:

> *That I may know Him, and the power of His resurrection, and the fellowship of His sufferings, being made conformable unto His death; if by any means I might attain unto the resurrection of the dead.*
> *Not as though I had already attained, either were already perfect: but I follow after, if that I may apprehend that for which also I'm apprehended of Christ Jesus.*
> *Brethren, I count not myself to have apprehended : but this one thing I do, forgetting those things which are behind, and reaching forth unto those things which are before, I press toward the mark for the **prize** of the **high calling** of God in Christ Jesus.*
> (Philippians 3:10-14 (KJ))

Paul realized that his salvation did not guarantee that he would be found worthy to take part in the **prize** of the **high calling**.

Paul knew that effort, on his part, was very necessary. He likened this quest to a race he was running, for which he knew had a very special prize.

He called this prize the high calling. The meaning of the words in the original Greek is very interesting. High means upward or on the top. Calling means invitation or calling. Paul might have been literally saying, *"I press toward the mark for the prize of the upward invitation or the top calling of God..."*

Paul's own striving for this special prize should be an example for every Christian to apply to their life. Living in the final days of the Church age, the believer needs to heed Paul's instruction with utmost care. If we fail to hit the mark to which Paul says we need to strive, the consequences may be very grave. In subsequent chapters, we will see that this upward calling is the promise of escaping the Tribulation period plus much more.

Chapter 5 – First Fruit Believers

Many of the parables Jesus used were founded upon agricultural pictures, since the stories presented principles that were readily known and understood.

One of the best examples of this is found in the fourteenth chapter of Revelation. It describes the harvest of the earth; but more importantly, it gives an overall outline of the entire Tribulation period.

The Lamb and 144,000

This outline has been obscured from most in the Church because of the assumption that the 144,000 mentioned in Revelation 7:1-8, are the same 144,000 described in Chapter 14 of Revelation.

Those described in Revelation 7, are clearly servants of God from the 12 tribes of Israel. Note what is put on their foreheads:

> *Do not harm the land or sea or the trees until we (angels) put a **seal** on the foreheads of the servants of our God. Then I heard the number of those who were sealed: 144,000 from all the tribes of Israel.*
> (Revelation 7:3-4)

The 144,000 are sealed by God's angels as a protection from the wrath to come. The seal of protection is put in their foreheads. Compare this to the foreheads of the 144,000 described in Revelation 14:1:

> *Then I looked, and there before me was the Lamb, standing on Mount Zion, and with him 144,000 who had HIS name and HIS FATHER'S name written on their foreheads.*

These two groups of 144,000 clearly have different details written on their foreheads. The Jewish servants have seals, while the 144,000 in chapter 14, have the name of Jesus and the name of God written on theirs.

There are also other characteristics which show that these are not the same 144,000. Those in chapter 14 are in heaven:

> *And I heard a sound from* **heaven** *like the roar of rushing waters and like a loud peal of thunder. The sound I heard was like that of harpists playing their harps. And they sang a new song* **before** *the* **throne** *and before the four living creatures and the elders...* (Revelation 14:2-3)

Those found in Revelation 14, are in heaven **before** the Tribulation begins (Rev. 14:6-7), while those described in Revelation 7:1-8, are sealed for protection from the wrath to come on the earth (see Revelation 9:4). The 144,000, of Revelation 7, are on the earth **in** the Tribulation, while the scene shown in Revelation 14, is of 144,000, before the heavenly throne **prior to** the hour of Judgment. This setting is also what is seen in Revelation 19:6:

> *After this I heard what sounded like a roar of a great multitude in* **heaven** *shouting...*
> *Then I heard what sounded like a great multitude, like the roar of rushing waters and like loud peals of thunder shouting:*
> *Hallelujah! For our Lord God Almighty reigns. Let us rejoice and be glad and give him glory! For the wedding of the Lamb has come, and His bride has made herself ready.* (Revelation 19:1,6-7)

Comparing Revelation 14 and 19, it is very clear the 144,000, that are described in chapter 14 are in fact in heaven and not on the earth. For final proof this group is not the same as the 144,000 Jewish servants of chapter 7, notice the following:

> *...No one could learn the song except the 144,000 who had **been redeemed from the earth**.* (Revelation 14:3)

This clearly identifies this group as an earthly remnant in heaven. They are 144,000 believers in Christ who have been taken from the earth prior to the Tribulation. They are a very special group of people:

> *These are those who did not **defile** themselves with women, for they kept themselves **pure**. They follow the Lamb wherever he goes. They were purchased from among men and offered as **FIRST FRUITS** to God and the Lamb. No lie was found in their mouths; they are **blameless**.* (Revelation 14:4-5)

Notice that this group had not **defiled** themselves, but were found **pure** and **blameless**. This sounds strikingly similar to the description of those individuals revealed in the last two chapters. Those found worthy of escaping the Tribulation period:

> Had **not defiled** their garment. (Revelation 3:4)
> Made every effort to be found **spotless, blameless**, and at **peace** with Him. (II Peter 3:14)
> Strengthened their hearts so they were found **blameless** and **holy**. (I Thessalonians 3:13)

From the foregoing, it shows that this group of 144,000, represent Christians who had made the necessary preparations and were found worthy before God. Those found worthy of escaping the Tribulation hour were found blameless, spotless and undefiled. Because of their pure condition, they were taken to heaven as a FIRST FRUIT offering to God.

First Fruits

This select group of Christians was purchased from the earth as a FIRST FRUITS offering. The Greek for purchased means: to go to the market. It is a picture of God coming to the earth to select His FIRST FRUITS from the entire crop.

The farmer would gather the early crop as soon as enough had become ripe. Later, after the whole fields had been ripened by the summer heat, the entire crop would be harvested. The season would then close with the vintage, and the grapes were crushed in the vineyard.

This is a remarkable picture of what God is trying to reveal to us in Revelation 14. With the understanding that this group of 144,000, is not the same as the 144,000 given in Revelation 7, the picture of the entire period of the Tribulation hour becomes clear (**please see Chart I**).

Pre-Trib & Post-Trib Correct

Below is an outline of several key events of the Tribulation period. It will be shown that both the pre-tribulation theory and the post-tribulation theory are partially correct. While both have parts that are right, they both have error that can cause the Christian great harm.

6 VISIONS OF REVELATION 14

1) FIRST FRUIT BELIEVERS - IN HEAVEN (v. 1-5)
2) HOUR OF JUDGEMENT HAS COME (v. 6-7)
3) BABYLON THE GREAT HAS FALLEN (v. 8)
4) PERSECUTION BY THE BEAST (v. 9-13)
5) JESUS RETURNS IN CLOUDS – FINAL HARVEST (v. 14-16)
6) VINTAGE - IN WINEPRESS OF GOD'S WRATH (verses 17-20)

Revelation 14, gives us a panoramic view of the entire Tribulation period. God placed this chapter immediately after the one that describes the reign of the two Beasts. It is, as if, God said, "Time out, Let's look at this whole thing in perspective." And a beautiful perspective it is. Let's focus on the main points the end-time Christians need to understand.

First, God shows that prior to the Hour of Judgement, He plans to remove His FIRST FRUIT believers to Heaven. What a glorious hope this is to those living in these final days. As we have seen in previous chapters, God promises to take those believers who are accounted worthy, out of the Tribulation hour that is coming to test the whole world. After we are removed, judgement begins. This is precisely what is pictured in this summary chapter of Revelation 14.

Notice that God only removes the FIRST FRUIT believers. Not all Christians are taken at first. This is the major problem with the pre-tribulation view of the Rapture. It says that all Christians will be Raptured. God's Word reveals that only God's FIRST FRUITS are taken before the hour of judgement begins.

This picture in Revelation 14, shows what has been discovered in previous chapters of this book. Escape from the Tribulation period is possible, but is conditional. It is not guaranteed for any Christian, but based upon the worthiness of each individual believer. Only those who are found **blameless, spotless**, and **holy**, and who have **not defiled** themselves, will be counted worthy to be included in the Rapture of FIRST FRUIT believers.

After God removes His select group, He then allows Judgement to begin. Revelation 14, then reviews the two main episodes: the destruction of Babylon the Great, and the persecution by the Beast. Then the last two visions of Revelation 14 review the final gathering of the harvest and the vintage.

Harvest

When the Tribulation period is about over, the Lord Jesus
Christ will return in the clouds:

> *I looked, and there before me was a white **cloud**. And
> seated on the **cloud** was one "like a son of man" with a
> crown of gold on his head and a sharp sickle in his
> hand. Then another angel came out of the temple and
> called in a loud voice to him who was sitting on the
> **cloud**, "Take your sickle and reap, because the time to
> reap has come, for the **harvest** of the earth is ripe.*
> (Revelation 14:14-15)

The Lord will return for the final harvest after the hour of
Judgement has come to a close. This also agrees with the
agricultural picture discussed earlier. The farmer gathered in his
First Fruits from the early crop and then waited for the rest of
the field to ripen at the end of the summer. When the summer
was over, he would harvest the remainder of the crop.

Vintage

The final vintage of the grape season is when the grapes are
trodden down in the winepress. This is remarkably pictured as
the final scene of Revelation 14:

> *The angel swung his sickle on the earth, gathered its
> grapes and threw them into the great winepress of
> God's wrath. They were trampled in the winepress
> outside the city, and blood flowed out of the press, rising
> as high as the horses' bridles for a distance of 1,600
> stadia. (180 miles).* (Revelation 14:19-20)

This sounds very similar to that final battle before the
Millennium: "*...He treads the winepress of the fury of the wrath
of God Almighty.*" (Revelation 19:15)

Revelation 14, ends with the final battle of Armageddon. The chapter thus provides a very good summary or outline of the major events that are scheduled to occur during the period of the Tribulation. The Rapture of FIRST FRUIT believers is clearly indicated as the event that must precede this Tribulation hour. We will now discover just how these FIRST FRUIT believers arrived in heaven.

Rightly Dividing The Word

The traditional verses used to show the Rapture are found in I Corinthians 15:51-52, and I Thessalonians 4:15-18. Later in this book, we will show that these verses will actually occur at the very end of the Tribulation period.

For all Pre-Tribulation followers, don't panic. There is still an escape before the Tribulation period begins. It has been there all along, but has been hidden. Remember that Paul taught us in II Timothy 2:15 (KJ): "Study to show thyself approved unto God, a workman that needeth not to be ashamed, rightly dividing the word of truth."

Most of the confusion over when the Rapture is to take place has resulted from the fact that we have not properly divided the Word of truth; and that includes this author, who asks for forgiveness. By following the various traditions that have been developed, we have all been lead astray from what God's wonderful Word has for us.

Snatched Up To God

Chapter 12 of the book of Revelation tells us the story of a woman who gives birth to a male child. Most have incorrectly divided this section of the Word of truth, and said that this male child is Christ. By so doing, we have missed a vital key that reveals when the Rapture takes place and who is actually taken in the Rapture. Let's see what we have been missing all along:

> *A great & wondrous sign appeared in heaven:*
> *a woman clothed with the sun, with the moon under her feet and a crown of twelve stars on her head. She was pregnant and cried out in pain as she was about to give birth. Then another sign appeared in heaven: an enormous red dragon with seven heads and ten horns and seven crowns on his heads. His tail swept a third of the stars out of the sky and flung them to the earth. The dragon stood in front of the woman who was about to give birth, so that he might devour her child the moment it was born.*
> *She gave birth to a son, a **MALE CHILD**, who will rule all the nations with an iron scepter.*
> *And her child was **snatched up** to God and to HIS throne.* (Revelation 12:1-5)

This male child has been interpreted to be Jesus Christ. This is based upon Scriptures which do show that Jesus will rule the nations with an iron scepter:

> *You will rule them with an iron scepter; you will dash them to pieces like pottery. (Psalm 2:8)*
> *Out of his mouth comes a sharp sword with which to strike down the nations. He will rule them with an iron scepter.* (Revelation 19:15)

It is clear that Jesus Christ will rule the nations with an iron scepter. But this is not enough evidence that the male child is in fact Jesus Christ.

Jesus Christ was born, then He died, and then He rose from the dead. This story of the male child shows him being born and then **snatched up** to the throne of God. If this child were Jesus

Christ, it would have said that the dragon killed the child, and then the child was taken to the throne of God. It can be seen, from this, that the male child could not possibly be Jesus Christ. If it is not Jesus Christ, then who could it be?

The Word of God beautifully answers this question for us, as we will see below.

Overcomers

The book of Revelation gives many descriptions of those Christians that live exemplary lives before God. Jesus called them: OVERCOMERS:

> *To him who overcomes, I will give the right to eat from the tree of life, which is in the paradise of God.* (Revelation 2:7)
> *...He who overcomes will not be hurt at the second death.* (Revelation 2:11)
> *To him who overcomes, I will give some of the hidden manna. I will also give him a white stone with a new name written on it, known only to him...* (Revelation 2:17)
> *To him who overcomes will, like them (those few in Sardis who have not defiled their garments), be dressed in white...* (Revelation 3:5)
> *"Him who overcomes I will make a pillar in the temple of my God. Never again will he leave it. I will write on him the name of my God and the name of the city of my God, the new Jerusalem, which is coming down out of heaven from my God; and I will also write on him my new name."* (Revelation 3:12)
> *To him who overcomes, I will give the right to sit with me on my throne, just as I overcame and sat down with my Father on His throne.* (Revelation 3:21)

> *To him who overcomes and does my will to the end, I will give authority over the nations--He will rule them with an iron scepter; he will dash them to pieces like pottery.* (Revelation 2:26 & 27)

As Christians, we are called to be overcomers. Not all Christians, however, are overcomers. Notice the description of the overcomers who are shown in the last listing: They will rule with Jesus Christ, *"with an iron scepter..."*

This is the precise description of the MALE CHILD, given in Revelation 12:5:

> *She gave birth to a son, a MALE CHILD, who will rule all the nations with an iron scepter.*
> *And her child was snatched up to God and to HIS throne.*

The male child will rule the nations with Jesus Christ with an iron scepter. This male child is the Christian who is an overcomer when Jesus returns to snatch him away. He is the FIRST FRUIT believer that God will gather before His throne in heaven before the final harvest.

This male child is a select group of believers who will be taken to the throne of God in heaven before the dragon has a chance to kill him. The Christian who is an overcomer and a FIRST FRUIT believer will be taken off of the earth to be with God before the devil has a chance to hurt him.

Notice how the Word of God beautifully connects the overcomer with those believers who are assured of missing the Tribulation:

> *To him who overcomes and does my will to the end...*
> (Rev.2:26)   COMPARED TO:

Because thou hast kept the word of my patience, I also
will keep thee from the hour of temptation...
(Revelation 3:10 (KJ))

Those overcomers who do God's will to the end or who keep
God's word are given the blessed promise of being kept from
going into the hour of testing.

Also, remember the overcomer (Revelation 3:12) has the name
of God and Jesus written on him. This harmonizes perfectly
with the FIRST FRUIT believers described in Revelation 14:1.
The FIRST FRUIT believer is the overcomer who has the
glorious assurance of not going into the Tribulation period. He
is the male child who is snatched up to the throne of God before
the dragon can harm him (**see Chart II for summary**).

Taken Out Of The Way

The above teaching is confirmed for us by Paul in his second
letter to the Thessalonians. In this chapter, Paul discusses the
timing of the Day of the Lord. He tells us:

Let no man deceive you by any means: for that day (Day
of the Lord) shall not come, except there come a falling
away first, and that man of sin (Antichrist) be revealed,
the son of perdition. (II Thessalonians 2:3 (KJ))

He says that the falling away will precede the Day of the Lord.
He also says that the Antichrist will be revealed before that day
comes. Notice, however, what is holding back the revelation of
the Antichrist:

And now you know the thing holding back, for him to be
revealed in his time. For the mystery of lawlessness
already works, only HE holding back now, until it comes
out of the midst; and then the Lawless One will be
revealed... (II Thessalonians 2:7- Inter-linear translation)

This might be paraphrased: "He is holding the Antichrist (who is already at work) from being revealed. When He is taken out of (or abundantly above) their midst, then the Antichrist will be revealed."

Most have interpreted the "He" in the above verses to represent the Holy Spirit. The theory states that the Holy Spirit is taken out through the Rapture of all Christians, and then the Antichrist is revealed.

The problem with this theory is the fact that the book of Revelation indicates that many people will be saved during the period of the Tribulation. If the Holy Spirit is taken out of their midst, it would be impossible for anyone to be saved after that.

The only possible explanation of who the "HE" is in the above verse is the male child that is found in Revelation 12:5. This fits in perfectly with what we have already learned. Once the male child is taken out of the way (Greek: abundantly above) then the Antichrist is revealed. The male child is snatched up to heaven, abundantly above the reach of the dragon. Both are beautiful pictures of how God plans to keep this select group from the hands of Satan. Only after He has removed His select overcoming first fruit believers, will He allow the Antichrist on stage.

Chart 1

	Revelation 7 144,000 JEWISH SERVANTS	Revelation 14 144,000 FIRST FRUIT BELIEVERS
DIFFERENT FOREHEADS	Seal of Protection (Revelation 7:3)	Identification Mark (Revelation 14:1)
DIFFERENT LOCATIONS	On the Earth during the Tribulation (Rev. 7:3-4 & 9:4)	In Heaven before the Tribulation (Rev. 14:1 & 14:7)
DIFFERENT PEOPLE	Tribes of Israel (Revelation 7:4)	Redeemed from the Earth (Rev. 14:3)
DIFFERENT ASSOCIATES	Living with Demon Locusts (Rev.9:3-4)	Living with the Lamb Jesus (Rev. 14:1)

Chart 2

	OVERCOMER	MALE CHILD	FIRST FRUIT BELIEVER
NAME ON FOREHEAD	"I will write on him the NAME of MY GOD and... MY NEW NAME" (Rev. 3:12)		"...144,000 who had HIS NAME and HIS FATHER'S NAME written on their foreheads." (Rev. 14:1)
IRON SCEPTER	"To him who OVERCOMES... he will RULE THEM with AN IRON SCEPTER." (Rev2:27)	"She gave birth to a MALE CHILD, who will RULE THEM with AN IRON SCEPTER." (Rev12:5)	
PRE-TRIB RAPTURE		"he was SNATCHED UP to God and to HIS THRONE." (Rev12:5)	"144,000...before the THRONE...were redeemed from the earth." (Rev. 14:1-5)
UNDEFILED	"...a few names... who have not DEFILED their garments ...they are worthy." (Rev. 3:4)		"...144,000...these are they which were not DEFILED..." (Rev.14:3&4)

Chapter 6 – Spiritual Earthquake

The stage is being set for one of the most devastating earthquakes mankind could ever imagine. This is not an earthquake that will shake the earth's crust or even the economy. The earthquake that is coming is going to be a SPIRITUAL EARTHQUAKE.

Earthquakes are generally felt in one area of the world at any given point. The spiritual earthquake that is coming, will be felt around the world at the same time. It will be one of the most horrifying events in history.

The majority of Christians believe in the pre-tribulation theory of the Rapture. This theory states that all born-again believers will be taken in the Rapture, to be with the Lord, before the Tribulation period begins. Let's look at some of the major "fault-lines" in this widely accepted theory.

Last Trumpet

I Corinthians 15:51-52, are some of the main verses used to show the pre-tribulation Rapture:

> *Behold, I show you a mystery; We shall not all sleep, but we shall all be changed, In a moment, in the twinkling of an eye, at the **last trumpet**: for the trumpet shall sound, and the dead shall be raised incorruptible, and we shall be changed.*

First of all, notice that Paul says the dead will be raised and the living changed at the last trumpet. When does the Word of God say the last trumpet will sound?

The book of Revelation answers this question for us. There are seven angels whose job it will be, to sound seven trumpets. The angels begin in Revelation 8:6, and continue until the last one is sounded in Revelation 11. Notice the events surrounding the sounding of the seventh or **last trumpet**:

> The **seventh angel** sounded his **trumpet**, and there were loud voices in heaven, which said: "The kingdom of the world has become the kingdom of our Lord and of his Christ, and he will reign for ever and ever.
> (Christ's reign of the world begins.)
> And the twenty-four elders, who were seated on their thrones before God, fell on their faces and worshiped God, saying: "We give thanks to you, Lord God Almighty, who is and who was, because you have taken your great power and have begun to reign. The nations were angry; and your wrath has come. The time has come for judging the dead, and rewarding your servants the prophets and your saints and those who reverence your name... (Revelation 11:15-18)

The timing of the seventh trumpet or the **last trumpet** occurs when Jesus returns to the kingdom of the world to begin His reign. It is at this time that He will begin His judgement. This time was also prophesied by Enoch in Jude 14-15(KJ):

> And Enoch also, the seventh from Adam, prophesied of these, saying, Behold the Lord cometh with ten thousands of his saints, to execute judgement upon all...

Notice, it is at this time that Jesus returns with His saints to execute judgement. This is the return of the Lord at the very end of the Tribulation period. For further proof the reader may want to read the description of Jesus Christ returning to the earth in Revelation 19:11-21.

The strong adherents to the pre-tribulation theory will argue that Paul said the last trumpet, but that it does not necessarily mean the last trumpet in the book of Revelation. While this argument has little basis, let's not argue; but let's look further into the words Paul used:

> *Behold, I show you a mystery; We shall not all sleep, but we shall all be changed, In a moment, in the twinkling of an eye, at the last trumpet: for the trumpet shall sound, and the **dead shall be raised** incorruptible, and we shall be changed.*
> (I Corinthians 15:51-52 (KJ))

Notice that Paul says the dead shall be raised at the sounding of the last trumpet. When will the dead be raised? The Word of God gives us a very clear answer with Daniel:

> *As for you (Daniel), go your way till the end. You will rest, and then at **the end of the days** you **will rise** to receive your allotted inheritance.* (Daniel 12:12)

It is very clear that the dead will not rise until the very end of the days. The last trumpet will sound when the dead rise from their graves. This clearly places the last trumpet at the end of the Tribulation period. To argue that the last trumpet will sound before the end of the days is completely unfounded.

IN THE AIR

The other key verses that are used to show the pre-tribulation view are found in I Thessalonians 4:15-17:

> *According to the Lord's own word, we tell you that we who are still alive, **who are left** till the coming of the Lord, will certainly not precede those who have fallen asleep. For the Lord himself will come down from heaven, with a loud command, with the voice of the archangel and with the trumpet call of God, and the dead in Christ will rise first. After that, we who are still*

*alive and **who are left** will be caught up with them **in the
clouds** to meet the Lord in the air. And so we will be
with the Lord forever.*

Notice where the above event takes place. It says **in the clouds**.
This is the exact same place that was described in the previous
chapter when the earth is harvested:

*I looked, and there before me was a white **cloud**. And
seated on the **cloud** was one "like a son of man" with a
crown of gold on his head and a sharp sickle in his
hand. Then another angel came out of the temple and
called in a loud voice to him who was sitting on the
cloud, "Take your sickle and reap, because the time to
reap has come, for the harvest of the earth is ripe."*
(Revelation 14:14-15)

This meeting in **the clouds** takes place near the very end of the
Tribulation period. Jesus is coming in the clouds to gather in the
whole harvest. This is the precise picture Paul was discussing in
I Thessalonians 4. For further proof that this is so, notice the
strong hint that Paul gave us in verses 15 and 17:

*...we tell you that we who are still alive, **who are left** till
the coming of the Lord...
...After that, we who are still alive and **who are left** will
be caught up...*

In both of these verses, Paul added the phrase: **who are left**, or
who remain. He could have just as easily left this out in both
places. Unless...unless he was trying to convey something very
important.

The Greek for this phrase is: *to leave all around, survive, or
remain.* By adding this phrase in both places, Paul was trying
to convey: some will remain, some will survive, some will be

left all around. Paul was implying that some would be taken previously to the time mentioned, and that those who had not been taken, but *who remain* will be taken at this time.

Through the Holy Spirit, Paul is implying that some will be taken earlier; and then those who were not taken earlier (but *who remain*) will be taken into the clouds to meet the Lord in the air.

This is precisely the scenario that has been developed thus far in this book. Some are taken in the Rapture of the First Fruit believers at first, followed by the final harvest of all who remain at the very end.

The First Fruits are taken to the **throne** of God in heaven, while the main harvest rapture is gathered in by the Lord when He returns on the **clouds** at the very end.

Cracks In Theory

The pre-tribulation theory is largely based upon the Scriptures that were outlined above. The pre-tribulation theory is believed by the majority of the Christian church and the majority of prophecy teachers and students.

We now see that there are some major cracks showing in this theory. These cracks can either be disregarded and ignored as utterly ridiculous, or they can be heeded by the leaders of the Church.

The severity of the COMING SPIRITUAL EARTHQUAKE will be determined by the spiritual condition of each individual believer. The leaders of the Church will be held responsible for their condition.

When the Rapture of the First Fruit believers takes place; many Christians, who believed in the pre-tribulation Rapture, will be utterly devastated. The grief will be overwhelming. The horror of having to face the testing of the Tribulation period will be dreadful.

Great Multitude

Most WHO REMAIN will be required to become martyrs for Christ. Some will be able to escape the wrath of the Antichrist, but the majority will have to give up their life in order to reach the Kingdom of heaven.

These facts are dramatically revealed to us in two places in Revelation:

> *After this I looked and there before me was a **great multitude** that no one could count, from every nation, tribe, people and language, standing before the throne and in front of the Lamb.*
> *...These are they who have **come out of the great tribulation**; they have **washed** their **robes** and made them white in the blood of the Lamb.*
> (Revelation 7:9&14)   AND
> *They overcame him (Antichrist) by the blood of the Lamb and the word of their testimony; they did not love their lives so much as to shrink from death.*
> (Revelation 12:11)

Notice the book of Revelation shows there will be a **great multitude** from every nation around the world. It will be a large group of people, too numerous to count. In all probability, this great multitude of born-again believers will be comprised of many of the Christians in our Churches today.

Soiled Robes

Notice that this group of Christians had to **wash** their **robes** in order to make them **white**. This tells us a great deal about them.

First of all, it tells us that they had white robes at one time, which means that they were indeed Christians (Isaiah 61:10).

Second, it tells us they somehow had gotten their robes dirty. This is a picture of the Christian too caught up with the things of this world. They had soiled their garments by not living the blameless, holy life they had been called to.

Remember those few in Sardis had not defiled their garments, and were able to walk with the Lord dressed in white because they were worthy. Had the great multitude heeded the Word of God, they would not have found themselves in the Tribulation period. They did not keep God's word, and were not kept from the time of testing.

Overcomer

Also notice this great multitude is finally required to become overcomers. In the last chapter, we saw that all Christians are called to be overcomers. Some were overcomers prior to the Tribulation period beginning. They were the First Fruit believers who had kept God's word and kept themselves undefiled. They were found blameless, holy and worthy before God; thereby proving to be overcomers in God's sight.

The great multitude, on the other hand, will enter into the Tribulation period because they have not been true overcomers prior to when it begins. They will finally become overcomers when they are required to stand up for Christ during the Tribulation hour. Their only hope at that point will be to die for Christ. They will have to refuse the mark of the beast and be martyred for Jesus.

SPIRITUAL EARTHQUAKE

Once the Rapture of First Fruit believers occurs, the Christians remaining will be completely surprised. Most had been taught all Christians are taken when the Rapture takes place. The horror of being left behind will be devastating. Blame, guilt and remorse will initially fill every believer's heart. The true Church that remains will need to come together like it has never done before.

Until the **SPIRITUAL EARTHQUAKE** occurs, the believer still has time to prepare. This message is an exhortation to all born-again believers to repent and prepare to meet the Bridegroom. There is still time to be included in the First Fruits Rapture. There is still time to keep God's word and be found holy, blameless, and worthy before God. Remember our Lord's instructions:

Watch...and pray always, that ye may be accounted worthy to escape... (Luke 21:36)

Chapter 7 – Upward Calling

In the fourth chapter we saw how the Apostle Paul was constantly striving for the **prize** of the **high calling**. This was seen in the verses which follow:

> *That I may know Him, and the power of His resurrection, and the fellowship of His sufferings, being made conformable unto His death; if by any means I might attain unto the resurrection of the dead.*
>
> *Not as though I had already attained, either were already perfect: but I follow after, if that I may apprehend that for which also I'm apprehended of Christ Jesus.*
>
> *Brethren, I count not myself to have apprehended: but this one thing I do, forgetting those things which are behind, and reaching forth unto those things which are before, I press toward the mark for the **prize** of the **high calling** of God in Christ Jesus.*
>
> (Philippians 3:10-14 (KJ))

Paul knew that he was saved by grace through faith in Jesus Christ. And yet, he knew that there was this high calling to which he was not guaranteed.

As we have seen, the Greek for this high calling means: high = upward or on the top, and calling = invitation or calling. Paul was seeking to obtain the upward invitation, or the top calling of God. He saw this as a prize to be won.

This is analogous to a runner in a race. Every participant strives to do their best in the hope of winning the top prize. No one is assured of that prize, and everyone strives to be the winner. In a race, there is always the possibility of stumbling or falling. The runner may not even be able to finish the race.

Paul recognized these possibilities, and tried to relay his sense of urgency to others. Notice his comments after talking about winning the prize:

> *All of us who are mature should take such a view of things. And if on some point you think differently, that too God will make clear to you.* (Philippians 3:15)

Paul realized not everyone would understand the meaning of this upward calling; but he knew that they should if they were mature. He is saying that the mature Christian should understand this upward calling. If they don't understand, they should ask God to make it clear to them.

Just what is this upward calling which Paul so eagerly sought?

Worthy of The Kingdom

In an earlier chapter, we saw where Paul constantly prayed for the worthiness of his disciples. This was shown in the following Scriptures:

> *Which is the manifest token of the righteous judgement of God, that ye **may be counted worthy** of the **Kingdom** of GOD, for which ye also suffer.* (II Thess. 1:5 (KJ))
> *Wherefore also we **pray always** for you, that our God **would count you worthy** of this calling...*
> (II Thessalonians 1:11 (KJ))

Paul knew that these disciples were indeed Christians. In fact, they were an exemplary Church (see I Thess. 1 and II Thess. 1:1-4). And yet, Paul constantly prayed that they may be counted worthy of the calling into the Kingdom of God. Although they were Christians, Paul constantly prayed that God might find them worthy of this calling.

Notice, Paul was also concerned about himself:

> *That I may know Him, and the power of His resurrection, and the fellowship of His sufferings, being made conformable unto His death; **if by any means I might attain** unto the resurrection of the dead.*
> (Philippians 3:10 KJ)

Paul knew he was saved, and that his eternal destiny was secure. And yet, he indicates his own doubt about attaining to this resurrection of the dead. (The Interlinear translation reads: resurrection *out of* the dead).

Paul realized that his salvation did not assure him this. Because he was not sure, he pressed on, as if in a race, to win the prize. Paul knew there was a very special resurrection out of the dead which he wanted to be counted worthy enough to participate in:

> *Brethren, I count not myself to have apprehended: but this one thing I do, forgetting those things which are behind, and reaching forth unto those things which are before, I **press toward the mark** for the **prize** of the **high calling** of God in Christ Jesus.*
> (Philippians 3:13-14 (KJ))

Jesus also taught that there would be those who would be WORTHY of this special **calling** which Paul so eagerly sought. This is found in Luke 20:35:

> *But those who are considered **worthy** of taking part in **that age** and in the resurrection from the dead...*

Jesus indicated that there would be a special group that would be considered worthy enough to participate in this resurrection from the dead. But notice He also indicated they would take part in a certain age. The Greek shows that this is a Messianic period or an age.

1,000 Year Reign

The first resurrection begins a period of 1,000 years. This is described in the book of Revelation:

> **Blessed** and **holy** is he that hath part in the first resurrection: on such the second death hath no power, but they shall be priests of God and of Christ, and shall reign with Him a thousand years.
> (Revelation 20:6 (KJ))

This indicates that those who take part in the first resurrection are considered blessed and holy. This shows it is for a special group of people. Could it be those who are considered worthy in God's sight? Let's see who is included in this first resurrection from the dead:

> I saw [1] **thrones** on which **were seated** those who had been given authority to judge. And I saw [2] the **souls** of those who had been **beheaded** because of their testimony for Jesus and because of the Word of God. They had not worshiped the beast or his image and had not received his mark on their foreheads or their hands. They came to life and reigned with Christ a thousand years.
> (Revelation 20:4)

Notice there are two groups in view here. The second group John saw were the **souls** who had been **martyred** for Jesus. Notice that only the souls were seen at first, and then they came to life to reign with Christ for 1,000 years. This places the first resurrection near the very beginning of the Millennium.

This second group represents those who died for Jesus during the Tribulation period. They are given the honor of reigning with Christ during the Millennium because of this.

The first group, however, consists of those who were **seated** on **thrones** with the authority to judge. We know from I Corinthians 6:2, that the saints are the ones who will judge the world. In the above scene, however, notice where this group is located. It says: **seated on thrones.**

We saw earlier in this book, that the overcomers are the ones who are seated on the throne with God:

> *To him who overcomes, I will give the right to **sit** with me on my **throne**, just as I overcame and sat down with my Father on His throne.* (Revelation 3:21)

Only the overcomers are given the right to sit on the throne with God. The group in view at the first resurrection includes those who were overcomers prior to when the Tribulation period began, plus those who through martyrdom became overcomers by the Word of their own testimony (Rev. 12:11).

The timing and purpose of this scene is also verified by Jude 14:

> *And Enoch also...prophesied of these, saying Behold, the Lord cometh with ten thousands of his saints, to execute judgement upon all...* (Jude 14 (KJ))

The first group mentioned as part of the first resurrection, represent the overcoming saints of God who will be given thrones from which they will have the authority to judge. While all saints are called to judge the world, only the overcomers and the martyrs are seen as part of the first resurrection.

Book of Life

If all saints are to judge the world, and only the overcomers and martyrs are included in the first resurrection, then when are the rest of the saints raised?

The only possible explanation is that they are resurrected at the end of the 1,000 year Millennium. This is described for us in Revelation 20:7, 11-15 (KJ). Pay particular attention to the last verse:

> And when the thousand years are expired, Satan shall be loosed out of his prison...
>
> And I saw a great white throne, and him that sat on it, from whose face the earth and the heaven fled away; and there was found no place for them. And I saw the dead, small and great, stand before God; and the books were opened: and another book was opened, which is the book of life: and the dead were judged out of those things which were written in the books, according to their works. And the sea gave up the dead which were in it; and death and hell delivered up the dead which were in them: and they were judged every man according to their works: And **whosoever was not found written in the book of life** was cast into the lake of fire.

The last verse indicates that whosoever was not included in the book of life was thrown into the lake of fire. This implies that there will be some at the end of the 1,000 years who will be present whose names **are** "*found written in the book of life.*"

This group of people must represent all those true born-again believers who were not found part of the first resurrection. Although they missed the 1,000 year reign with Christ, their names were found written in the book of life, and they were not thrown into the lake of fire.

These Christians were indeed saved, and their names could never be erased from the book of life. They missed the Rapture of First Fruit believers because they were not considered worthy by the Lord. Once they entered into the Tribulation period they could have participated in the first resurrection by becoming martyrs. The fact they did not become martyrs indicates they must have died before they had a chance to be martyred. This is highly probable, knowing that over 3 billion people will die during the Tribulation period.

Excluded From the Kingdom

The Word of God does indicate that there will be Christians who do not enter into this 1,000 year reign with Christ:

> *Not everyone who says to me, "Lord, Lord," will enter the Kingdom of heaven, but only he who does the will of my Father who is in heaven.* (Matthew 7:21)

The fact these people called Jesus, "Lord" indicates that they were Christians (please see I Corinthians 12:3). This indicates that there will be Christians who will not enter into the 1,000 year reign with Christ, known as the Kingdom of heaven. This is that upward calling which Paul so fervently sought.

Many of the other parables Jesus taught also indicate there will be some Christians who are excluded from reigning with Christ during the Kingdom. The reader may want to read: Matthew 25:1-30, & Luke 13:22-30, for examples of this teaching. Please keep in mind that exclusion from the Kingdom of heaven does not mean exclusion from Heaven.

Worthy of Upward Calling

Remember that Jesus taught there are those who are considered worthy of participating in the kingdom age (Luke 20:35):

> *But those who are considered **worthy** of taking part in **that age** and in the resurrection from the dead...*

There is a group of believers God considers worthy of participating in the future kingdom during the Millennium. This is a select group of born-again believers who please God.

Also remember those who take part in this resurrection are called: *"blessed and holy"* (see Revelation 20:6). These words were written by the Apostle John. One of John's disciples was named Polycarp, who contributed the following to this subject:

> *If we **please** Him in this present age, we shall also receive the Age to Come; and if we **walk worthy** of Him, we shall also **reign** together with Him.*

Polycarp's insight seems to parallel what has been brought out in this book. Those who please God by living holy and blameless lives in this present time will be found worthy of the wonderful privilege of reigning with Christ in the Millennium.

Upward Calling

Those first fruit believers who are overcomers will be considered blessed and holy and worthy to take part in the first resurrection and the 1,000 year reign with Christ.

While the first resurrection will include both the first fruit overcomers and the martyrs of the Tribulation period, the high calling is to be included in the first fruit group, and thereby escape the Tribulation entirely. Both are included in the first resurrection, but the former group represents the upward calling which Paul so fervently sought. The value of praying the way Jesus taught us to pray brings on added importance:

> *Watch ye therefore, and pray always, that ye may be accounted worthy to escape all these things that shall come to pass, and to stand before the Son of man.*

By praying the above prayer, with a heartfelt desire, God will provide a way for those who are truly sincere and committed to His Word. By the power of His Spirit, they will escape the Tribulation and be included in the first resurrection. To be included is truly the ***Upward Calling*** all should earnestly strive and pray.

Chapter 8 – Final Preparations

We have seen that a potentially devastating *SPIRITUAL EARTHQUAKE* is about to hit! Once it arrives, there will be no turning back. People will not be given another chance. God will remove the First Fruit believers who are prepared and ready to meet Him. Those found walking with Him and worthy in His sight will have the glorious privilege of being with Him.

All others will be faced with the horrors of the Tribulation. After the Rapture of First Fruit believers takes place, the Antichrist will be revealed (II Thes.2:7-8), and he will perform all kinds of counterfeit miracles with great signs and wonders. He will appear to be Christ, but he will be a counterfeit.

Many professing or nominal Christians will follow him. Notice why:

> *The coming of the lawless one will be in accordance with the work of Satan displayed in all kinds of counterfeit miracles, signs and wonders, and in every sort of evil that deceives those who are perishing. They perish because they refused to love the truth and be saved.*
>
> *For this reason God sends them a powerful delusion so that they will believe the lie and so that all will be condemned who have not believed the truth but have delighted in wickedness.* (II Thessalonians 2:9-12)

Those who do not truly love the truth will be sent a very strong delusion from God!

Church Shaken

God will truly shake the Church after His First Fruit believers are taken from this planet. Those merely professing to be

Christians will follow the lie and the work of Satan.

However, there will be a great multitude of real Christians remaining. These will be truly born-again believers who failed to prepare to meet the Bridegroom. They will recognize the Antichrist for who he really is, and they will not follow him.

After the shattering **EARTHQUAKE**, the greatest aftershock to follow will be when these very Christians realize they were misled. They were not taken in the Rapture because their Pastors and Teachers (who should have known) failed in their duties as Watchmen and taught false doctrine. That is why Jesus urged His disciples not to be led astray by any man (Matthew 24:4).

Their anger, remorse and regret will need to be put behind them quickly. The Church will need to come together to help and encourage one another. They will now be faced with the reality that martyrdom will probably be required of them. Those days will be some of the most perilous times one could imagine. If they are not killed by war first, they will become those described in Revelation 12:11:

> *They overcame him by the blood of the Lamb and by the word of their testimony; they did not love their lives so much as to shrink from death.*

People will be required to receive a mark on their right hand or forehead. The only other alternative will be death. The true Christian will stand up for Jesus and refuse to receive the mark. They will be killed, but they will be assured of going to be with the Lord. If they receive the mark, they seal their fate:

> *If anyone worships the beast and his image and receives his mark on the forehead or on the hand, he, too, will drink of the wine of God's fury, which has been*

poured full strength into the cup of his wrath. He will be tormented with burning sulfur in the presence of the holy angels and of the Lamb. (Revelation 14:9-10)

TIME TO PREPARE

If you are reading this book prior to when the Rapture takes place, you still have time to prepare to take part in it. You are probably in one of the following categories:

1) Unrighteous and lost.
2) Professing Christian.
3) Born-again with defiled garments.
4) First Fruit prepared believer.

Unrighteous and Lost

If you do not know Jesus Christ as your Lord and Savior, and you are reading this book, you need to come to a personal relationship with Him now. Jesus came and died for your sins that you might not have to pay the penalty. He not only died for your sins, but He also rose from the dead. He conquered death so that you might live. You need to believe on the Lord Jesus Christ as your own personal Savior. Why not make the following acknowledgment in your heart right now:

Dear God in Heaven, I don't fully understand everything about this, but I know that I am a sinner and that I need a Savior. Thank You for sending Your Son, Jesus to die for my sins and pay the penalty. By faith I come to You now Lord and ask You to save me. Help me to live the remainder of my life for You, being led by Your Holy Spirit. Please count me worthy to escape all that is about to happen on this earth. In the precious name of Jesus Christ, I pray. Amen.

If you sincerely prayed this prayer, praise the Lord! He has saved you by the precious blood of Jesus Christ. You will want to make sure that you follow through with the above prayer by reading His Word and praying to Him every day. Find a church where the Word of God is preached, and be sure to tell others about your new faith in Jesus Christ and the fact that He is coming back again very soon!

Professing Christian

If you profess Jesus Christ as your personal Savior, are you keeping His word? Are you walking as Christ did?

> *Now by this we know that we know Him, if we keep His commandments. He who says, "I know Him," and does not keep His commandments, is a liar, and the truth is not in him. But whoever keeps His word, truly the love of God is perfected in Him. By this we know that we are in Him. He who says he abides in Him ought himself also to walk just as He walked.* (I John 2:4-6 (NKJV)

There are many people who profess to be born-again believers. Only Christ knows their hearts and whether or not they have acknowledged the Lord Jesus Christ in their heart. If upon examining your heart, in all honesty, you realize you are not truly a Christian, humbly acknowledge Him right now by re-reading the previous page. Believing on the Lord Jesus Christ is the most important decision of your life. True salvation only requires believing on the Lord Jesus Christ and acknowledging Him as your own personal Savior.

Born-Again With Defiled Garments

The book of Revelation indicates that there will be a great multitude of believers who will be required to become martyrs (please see Revelation 7:9-17). This portion of the Word of God tells us that there will be many born-again believers who will enter the horror of the Tribulation period. They were Christians before it began because they had their robes. The reason they were required to go into the Tribulation period is shown in verse 14: *"They have washed their robes and made them white in the blood of the Lamb."*

These born-again believers had soiled their garments and needed to wash them to make them white again. They were not as careful as the few found in the church of Sardis:

> *Thou hast a few names even in Sardis which have not defiled their garments; and they shall walk with me in white: for they are worthy.* (Revelation 3:4 (KJ))

These few in Sardis had kept their garments white and were found worthy. These are the First Fruit believers that made the necessary preparations by walking with the Lord in obedience to His Word. They are the overcomers who pleased God and were found looking for Him when the Rapture took place.

For those readers who are born-again with defiled garments, let's look at the preparations that are required in order to be found worthy; and some attributes of First Fruit believers.

FIRST FRUIT BELIEVERS

Keep God's Word

Revelation 3:10, reminds us:

> *Because thou hast kept the word of my patience, I also will keep thee from the hour of temptation, which shall come upon all the world, to try them that dwell upon the earth.*

The believer who is obedient to God's word is given the wonderful promise of escaping the Tribulation period.

Walk In Light

I John 1:7, instructs us: *But if we walk in the light, as he is in the light, we have fellowship with one another, and the blood of Jesus, his Son, purifies us from all sin.*

The believer needs to walk in the light as opposed to walking in darkness. This means that the believer should separate themselves from any sin. If there is any sin in the life of the believer, they should repent (turn away from it) and ask for forgiveness from the Lord:

> *If we confess our sins, he is faithful and just and will forgive us our sins and purify us from all unrighteousness.* (I John 1:9)

Please God

The First Fruit believers are protégé's of Enoch who was described in Hebrews 11:5:

> *...For before he was taken (Raptured), he was commended as one who* ***pleased*** *GOD.*

The believer will want to please the Lord by the life that they live. The motives of the First Fruit believer will always be to please God.

Witness

One other big lesson that can be learned from Enoch is that the believer should be actively witnessing to others that Jesus is getting ready to return. Notice what is said of Enoch in Jude 14:

> *And Enoch also, the seventh from Adam, prophesied of these, saying, behold, the Lord cometh with ten thousands of his saints.*

Telling others to come to the Lord and the fact that JESUS IS COMING very soon is a very important part in the life of the believer. The Word of God says very little about Enoch. What is does say should be listened to very carefully. Telling others the Lord is coming is very important.

Persevere

The believer needs to remember the example of Paul who always *"pressed toward the mark for the prize of the high calling."* Paul was diligent and he persevered until the end of his life. The believer worthy of this prize will heed the Lord's words in Luke 9:62:

> *Jesus replied, No one who puts his hand to the plow and looks back is fit for service in the kingdom of God.*

By not looking back the Lord means living their lives the way they used to live before they were saved. Many born-again believers have returned to living their lives the way they were before salvation. The church has gotten so lukewarm, that there is very little difference between the world and the Church.

The believer will want to remember the story of Lot's wife. She had grown too attached to the place she was leaving. She didn't really want to leave it. She looked back, and was destroyed. The believer should not grow too attached to this world. Their real home is in heaven, but too many believers are looking back. They need to repent and stop being friends with this world. Remember Lot's wife and remember the words of James:

> *Anyone who chooses to be a friend of the world becomes an enemy of God.* (James 4:4)

Be Humble

The believer will want to remember that true humility is something to be highly valued:

Blessed are the poor in spirit: for theirs is the kingdom of heaven. (Matthew 5:3 (KJ))

The humble believer is given the wonderful assurance by our Lord that their inheritance is the Kingdom of heaven.

Be Holy

Holiness is a major ingredient that is missing from the Church today. The believer should make sure they are living a holy life:

> **Make every effort** *to live in peace with all men and to* **be holy***; without holiness no one will see the Lord.* (Hebrews 12:14)

It is the responsibility of every believer to heed these words. For those believers who have not been living holy lives, they should repent and begin leading holy lives from here on, until the Lord returns.

Be Blameless

In line with holiness, the believer needs to make every effort to be blameless and pure:

> *So then, dear friends, since you are looking forward to this,* **make every effort** *to be found* **spotless***,* **blameless** *and at* **peace** *with him.* (II Peter 3:14)

While the believer will not reach spotless perfection until the Lord returns, the born-again believer should be making every effort to be blameless and pure. It is the attitude and the motive of the heart that will determine if a person is making the effort required to have them found blameless. God knows those who are trying to please Him by looking into their heart.

BE WATCHFUL

The Word of God is filled with examples that teach the believer to be looking for and eagerly expecting the return of the Lord. A few of these are outlined below:

> ...*You ought to live holy and godly lives as you look forward to the day of God*... *So then, dear friends, since you are looking forward to this*...
> (II Peter 3:11&14)
> *But our citizenship is in heaven. And we eagerly await a Savior from there, the Lord Jesus Christ*...
> (Philippians 3:20)
> *Looking for that Blessed Hope.* (Titus 2:13)
> *Be always on the watch*... (Luke 21:36)
> *...and unto them that look for Him shall he appear the second time*... (Hebrews 9:28)

The above is only a very small sample of some of the Scriptures telling the believer to be alert and watching for the Lord to return. The Lord commanded the believer to always be on the watch. He is returning for those believers who are eagerly waiting and looking for Him.

Be Prayerful

Finally, the believer will realize that being found worthy to be included as part of the First Fruit group rests in the hands of the Lord. Because of this, Jesus instructed His humble followers to pray:

> *Watch ye therefore, and PRAY ALWAYS, that ye may be accounted worthy to escape all these things that shall come to pass, and to stand before the Son of man.*
> (Luke 21:36(KJ)

The believer realizes that being found worthy to escape the Tribulation depends upon the grace and mercy of the Lord. The believer will make every effort to be obedient to Him, and will humbly pray to be considered worthy.

Final Preparations

Until the cataclysmic **SPIRITUAL EARTHQUAKE** occurs, the reader can be included in the select group of First Fruit believers.

Remember the story of the thief dying on the cross next to Jesus:

> *And he said unto Jesus, LORD, remember me when thou comest into thy kingdom. And Jesus said unto him, Verily I say unto thee, Today shalt thou be with me in paradise.* (Luke 23:42-43(KJ))

This story is a beautiful example of the love and mercy of our Lord. Right up until the very time that this thief was about to die, this thief was lost. Then, he realized who Jesus was. He humbly asked Jesus to remember him. He called Him Lord. He was saved at the very last moment and given the assurance of being with Jesus.

In a similar manner, the person reading this book has the chance to humbly turn to Jesus and ask Him to count him worthy of escaping the horrible times ahead. Why not pray the following prayer right now:

> Dear God in Heaven, please help me to live my life in such a way that it is pleasing to you. Please consider me worthy to escape the time that is coming to test this world. In the name of Jesus, my Lord, I pray. Amen.

If you prayed the above prayer with a humble heart, you have made the most essential preparations to meet Him. Now, continue living for Him in holiness and looking for Him until He returns (I John 2:28).

Epilogue

A s I finish this work, the Lord reminded me of His words spoken through the prophet Habakkuk:

> *Write down the revelation and make it plain on tablets so that a herald [or; so that whoever reads it] may run with it.* (Habakkuk 2:2)

It is my prayer that I have made the message clear to those who have "eyes to see" and "ears to hear." It is up to you now to heed this message and to tell others while there is still time.

The vast majority of people will not understand, but the wise will understand. The current Church of Laodicea needs to be reminded:

> *If my people, who are called by my name, will humble themselves and pray and seek my face and turn from their wicked ways, then will I hear from heaven and will forgive their sin and will heal their land.* (II Ch. 7:14)

May God use this message to wake-up and prepare His people to meet Him.

30th Anniversary Abridged Edition

Since this book was originally written 30 years ago, we are rapidly approaching the time of the *Coming Spiritual Earthquake*. The words of Apostle Paul ring truer than ever:

> *1) But know this, that in the last days perilous times will come: 2) For men will be lovers of themselves, lovers of money, boasters, proud, blasphemers, disobedient to parents, unthankful, unholy, 3) unloving, unforgiving, slanderers, without self-control, brutal,*

> *despisers of good, 4) traitors, headstrong, haughty,*
> *lovers of pleasure rather than lovers of God, 5) having a*
> *form of godliness but denying its power. And from such*
> *people turn away!* (II Timothy 3:1-5 – NKJV)

The Apostle's striking description certainly portrays our present time, signifying these indeed must be the last of the last days. As such, time is rapidly running out and the final grains of sand are about to pass through the hour glass.

One of the main reasons why the Lord has not returned as of yet could be that He wants all believers to repent:

> *The Lord is not slack concerning His promise, as some*
> *count slackness, but is longsuffering **toward us**, not*
> *willing that any should perish but that all should **come***
> ***to repentance.*** (II Peter 3:9 – NKJV)

Apostle Peter indicates that what may appear to be slackness is really because the Lord does not want His people to perish in the coming Tribulation period. Peter indicates that if Christians will repent in time, they can be spared.

May we all take advantage of this extended period of grace to re-examine our lives and be led into a deeper repentance – in order to be that Holy bride without spot or blemish that our Bridegroom is returning for.

> *...that He might present her to Himself a glorious*
> *church, not having spot or wrinkle or any such thing,*
> *but that she should be holy and without blemish.*
> (Ephesians 5:27 – NKJV)

Time is running out. The severity of the *Coming Spiritual Earthquake* is about to be determined.

Appendix A – Questions & Answers

INDEX OF F.A.Q. (CONTINUED)
(Frequently Asked Questions)   Page

QUESTION A – Revelation 14, shows only 144,000 First Fruit believers. How many people are included in the Rapture of First Fruit believers?

ANSWER:
A literal interpretation of the Greek in Revelation 14:1, would mean 144,000. The question then becomes: should this passage be taken literally, or should it be considered symbolic?

Since Greek rules of grammar dictate that symbolic and literal elements are not mixed within the same verse, the 144,000 should properly be interpreted as being symbolic since Mount Zion is properly interpreted as symbolic of the heavenly Jerusalem.

The number of 144,000 was used to show that the number of First Fruit believers is in fact limited. While the number is limited, the total number in the Rapture is open and will hopefully be a great multitude.

QUESTION B – Jude 14, shows only 10,000 saints returning with Jesus. Is that all who will be Raptured?

ANSWER:
First, let's review what Jude 14 says:

> *And Enoch also, the seventh from Adam prophesied of these, saying, behold the Lord cometh with ten thousands of his saints.* (Jude 14 (KJ))

The above quote was taken from the King James version. The New International version says, *"with thousands upon thousands of his holy ones."* Let's look at the Interlinear Bible which is a more literal translation of the original Greek:

> *And Enoch, the seventh from Adam, also prophesied to these men, saying, Behold, the Lord came with myriads of His saints.*

The Greek uses the word: ***murias*** (#3611) which means: ten thousand or a myriad number or indefinite number. This same word (#3611) is used in Acts 19:19, and Revelation 9:16. In both of these cases, it means a literal 10,000. However, in Hebrews 12:22, this same word is used to mean "myriads" or an indefinite number. While *murias* could be either 10,000 or an indefinite number, it is worthy of noting that I Enoch may provide some insight.

Scholars believe that Jude 1:14-15 is the same judgement found in I Enoch 1:9, which states: *Behold, he will arrive with ten million of the holy ones.*

We believe a myriad number of Saints will be returning with the Lord and not just 10,000. May the Lord reach myriads of Saints with the message of this book to help sway the issue that an untold number of Saints will be returning with Him.

QUESTION C – What is the *"falling away"* in II Thessalonians 2:3?

ANSWER:
II Thessalonians 2:3(KJ), says:

> *Let no man deceive you by any means: for that day (Day of the Lord) shall not come, except there come a falling away first, and that man of sin be revealed, the son of perdition (Antichrist),*

This is saying that the falling away and the revelation of the Antichrist will occur before the Day of the Lord begins. However, before the Antichrist is revealed, remember that *"He"* must be taken out of the way. From chapter 5, we saw that this *"He"* is the **male child** of Revelation 12:5, or the Overcoming First Fruit believers. Only after they are Raptured, may the Antichrist be revealed. (See II Thessalonians 2:6-8)

But what about the "falling away," what is Paul referring to? The Greek word that is used is: *apostasia* (#646). This means defection, falling away, or to forsake. From this, many have felt Paul was referring to a falling away from the faith. This is also talked about in I Timothy 4:1. If this falling away from the faith is what Paul meant, it appears that it has begun and is continuing. Sound doctrine is no longer upheld by many and various "doctrines of devils" have permeated the church.

While the above interpretation may be right, there is another possibility. In seven of the first English translations before the King James Version, the word: apostasia is translated as: *"departynge"*. This would mean that Paul was saying that the departure must occur first. Or that the Rapture must happen before the Day of the Lord begins. This is in line with what has been shown in this book, and probably is a better exegesis of this passage.

QUESTION D – In Revelation 12, who is the "Woman"? and the "rest of her offspring" (v.17)?

ANSWER:
The "Woman" of Revelation 12:1, appears to be Israel (please see Genesis 37:9-10). She is the one responsible for the birth of the Church. Through Israel, Christ was born, and Christ is the

head of the Church (also read Rom. 9:4-5 & Colossians 1:18).

In chapter 5, we saw that the *male child* the woman gave birth to is the overcoming First Fruit believer. For further proof of this, notice who "the rest of her offspring" are:

> *And the dragon was wroth with the woman, and went to make war with the **remnant of her seed**, which **keep the commandments** of God, **and** have the **testimony of Jesus Christ**.* (Revelation 12:17(KJ))

In this story, Satan goes after Israel but is unable to harm her (see verse 14). He then goes after the woman's offspring. In verse 17, we see that her offspring are the remnant of Christians remaining. This ties the "*offspring*" with the *male child*. They were both born from the same mother: the "woman" described earlier. The "offspring" are pictured as believers which means that they could not be a Jewish remnant. They are Christians being pursued by the Antichrist during the Tribulation. They were directly related to the *male child,* having the same mother: the "woman."

The above explanation further enhances the argument that the *male child* is the First Fruit believer. He is pictured as one of the offspring's from the "woman" which means he is directly related to the "other offspring." The First Fruit believers are directly related to the Christians who will enter the Tribulation to be pursued by the Antichrist.

----------------◇◆◇----------------

QUESTION E – What is the "Mystery of God" described in Revelation 10:7?

ANSWER:
Revelation 10:7, says:

*But in the days when the **seventh** angel is about to **sound** his **trumpet**, the MYSTERY of God will be accomplished, just as he announced to his servants the prophets.*

This occurs when the seventh trumpet or the "last trumpet" is about to sound. In context with Revelation 11:15-19, this is at the very end of the Tribulation. Notice that it says the "*mystery of God*" is accomplished as told to God's servants. This mystery was hidden, but then revealed:

...according to the dispensation of God which is given to me for you, to fulfill the Word of God; Even the MYSTERY which hath been hid from ages & from generations but now is made manifest to his saints.

To whom God would make known what is the riches of the glory of this MYSTERY among the Gentiles; which is Christ in you, the hope of glory:
(Colossians 1:25-27(KJ))

This MYSTERY is the mystery of God working in the Gentiles, reconciling men to Himself. Paul also spoke of it:

...the MYSTERY made known to me by revelation...you will be able to understand my insight into the MYSTERY of Christ, which was not made known to men in other generations as it has now been revealed by the Spirit of God's holy apostles and prophets. (Ephesians 3:3-6)

This mystery is that through the gospel the Gentiles are heirs together with Israel, members together of one body, and sharers together in the promise of Christ Jesus. This mystery is clearly the mystery of God working in history, bringing both Jews and Gentiles together in Christ. Revelation 10, says when the seventh trumpet sounds, this mystery will be finished. This final dispensation of God will be over, and the Millennium will begin.

One other reference that Paul made to this MYSTERY is found in I Corinthians 15:51-52:

> *Behold, I show you a MYSTERY, We shall not all sleep, but we shall all be changed in a moment, in the twinkling of eye, at the LAST TRUMP; for the TRUMPET shall SOUND, and the dead shall be raised incorruptible, and we shall be changed.*

This traditional pre-tribulation verse ties in perfectly with Revelation 10:7. Both indicate the last trumpet will sound and both speak of the MYSTERY of God.

From the foregoing, the MYSTERY of God will be accomplished when the Tribulation period comes to an end at the sounding of the last trumpet. The MYSTERY of God bringing Jews and Gentiles together in Christ will be complete.

QUESTION F – Who is the bride of Christ? Please explain what the Word of God has to say.

ANSWER:
Who is the bride of Christ? When asked this question, almost everyone answers, "the Church," or "the body of Christ," meaning all saved people. However, nowhere in the Bible is the Church called the Bride of Christ. The Church is called His body in Ephesians 1:22-23, but the body and the bride are not synonymous as has been supposed.

Using the "rule of first mention," and keeping in mind that the things written in the Old Testament are types and examples for our learning (Romans 15:4, 1Cr 10:11), we can see that the bride is taken out of the body. Two examples from the Old Testament illustrate this truth: The first bride Eve was not the body of Adam, but was taken out of his body. Adam is a type of Christ. Eve is a type for the bride.

In Genesis 24 we have the story of Abraham who sent his servant to take a bride for his son, Isaac. Most people say this is a type for God the Father sending the Holy Spirit into the world for calling out the Church. However, this is not the true meaning of the story. While the Gospel is to go into all the world, in this story Abraham told the servant not to go to the Canaanites, but to go to his own people to take a bride for his son.

The correct interpretation is this: Abraham, a type of the Father, sent the servant, a type of the Holy Spirit, to his own people, a type of the Church, to take a bride for his son Isaac, a type of Christ. When the message of salvation goes forth, it goes to everyone; but when God calls for His bride, He calls not the world, but His own people, or His family.

Our Lord used the term "family" because of its meaning to us in our physical life. We are born the first time into a physical family. When we believe on the Lord Jesus Christ, trusting Him Who died in our place, we are born again, into the family of God. The bore "bride" is used in a similar sense. We know what the blessings of family life involve. We also know the bride and groom share a closeness and an intimacy, which is not shared by the other members of the family.

With these thoughts in mind, we can see how the Lord calls those who are His to come up closer. *"I beseech you therefore, brethren, by the mercies of God, that ye present your bodies a living sacrifice, holy, acceptable unto God which is your reasonable service.* ***And be not conformed to this world: but be ye transformed by the renewing of your mind****, that ye may prove what is that good and acceptable and perfect will of God"* (Romans 12:1-2).

Not many Christians heed this direct command. Many who are saved continue to conform to this world, and they never experience sweet communion and fellowship with the Lord Jesus; and like Esau, forfeit spiritual rewards in the future for gratification of the carnal nature in the present.

In writing to the carnal Corinthians, Paul tells them they are espoused to one husband, that is, they are promised in marriage or engaged. The word espoused is a very similar word used in Matthew 1:18, where Mary is espoused to Joseph. Before they came together he thought of putting her away since he thought she had been unfaithful. Many believers today may be unfaithful, and there is a sense in which the Lord may *"put them away."*

This does not mean the loss of their salvation, but in Rev 16:15, we read, *"Behold I come as a thief. Blessed is he that watcheth, and keepeth his garments lest he walk naked and they see his shame."* This refers not to His righteousness with which He clothes us for our own salvation (Isaiah 61:10), but to a garment of good works (deeds) which may be maintained with a profitable result, or which lost to our shame and loss of rewards when Jesus returns (1John 2:28, Titus 3:8, 2 John 1:8).

Revelation 19:7 says the bride *"**makes herself ready**"* for her soon marriage by providing a garment of good deeds. Many Christians do not live for Christ after they are saved and they are not preparing themselves to meet the Bridegroom.

Paul compared the Christian life to a race where all run, but only one receives the "**prize**" (1 Cor. 9:24-27). Paul was fearful that he would become a *"castaway,"* so he worked diligently to keep his body in subjection. In chapter three of Philippians, Paul talks about losing all things so that he might *"**gain Christ.**"* He also says that he wants to *"know Him and the power of His resurrection, and the fellowship of His sufferings, being conformed to his death, if, by any means, I may attain to the* *resurrection from the dead"* (Philippians 3:10-11 – NKJV).

The resurrection Paul is talking about in this passage of Scripture is something that is earned. It refers to a partial resurrection of Christians who have attained to a certain standard. Hebrews 11:35 calls it the *"better resurrection."* In the above passage of Scripture Paul emphasizes that he is working very hard to win the **"prize**," which is in Christ Jesus. The prize is clearly the highest reward that a believer can receive for faithful, spirit-filled service in the Lord's work. The Scriptures are replete with types, parables and doctrinal statements that express the honor and blessing attached to those who are part of the wedding of the Lord Jesus Christ.

Revelation 3:18 tells us to buy white raiment that we may be clothed and that the shame of our nakedness not appear. The white raiment is *"the righteous acts and deeds"* of the Saints. The word *"buy"* is used to show that it will cost the child of God to be among those who make up the Bride of Christ. A separated and surrendered life is costly, but how great will be the reward for those who dare to pay the price.

Many Christians are not doing these things and may not be part of the bride. We will all give an account of our lives and be rewarded according to the good and bad we have done (please read 2 Corinthians 5:10). Some do not live for the Lord and may suffer the loss of rewards. Those who have not provided themselves with a wedding garment may be spiritually naked and ashamed when the Lord returns.

Salvation is a free gift of God. It is eternal and cannot be lost. Crowns, rewards and an inheritance into the Kingdom are based upon faithfulness to Him. To be part of the Bride of Christ is a great reward to those Christians who have paid the price. It is a figurative picture of those who have lived a clean, pure, and holy life yielded to Him.

Just as any bride would prepare herself for her earthly bridegroom, so should every Christian prepare themselves to meet their heavenly Bridegroom. Just as a bride would not wear blue jeans to her wedding, the Bride of Christ will not be an average lukewarm Christian (read the warning to the Church of Laodicea (Revelation 3:14-22).

The Church is one body, made up of all believers in Christ. Some are spiritual and some are carnal (I Corinthians 3). As outlined in Matthew 25:1-13, some are wise and some are foolish. Who then is the bride?

Those who are providing themselves with a wedding garment and those who are preparing to meet the Bridegroom when He returns, as evidenced by their pure and sincere devotion to Jesus. All Christians will not qualify to be the bride. Will you?

One of the main purposes of this book is to help you prepare for the great Wedding that is about to occur. Please visit our website for more help in preparing to meet the Bridegroom when He returns for His beloved bride.

QUESTION G – When do the martyred saints in Revelation 7, get resurrected?

ANSWER:
The resurrection of the martyred saints is recorded in Revelation 20:4-5:

> *I saw thrones on which were seated those who had been given authority to judge. And I saw the souls of those*

who had been beheaded because of their testimony for Jesus and because of the Word of God. They had not worshiped the beast or his image and had not received his mark on their foreheads or their hands. **They came to life** *and reigned with Christ a thousand years... ...This is the first resurrection...*

Notice that at first, John only saw the First Fruit believers seated on their thrones along with the SOULS of the martyred saints. This tells us that the First Fruit believers had previously risen.

Then John saw the martyred saints come to life. This is part of the first resurrection. This occurs at the end of man's 6,000 years and right before the 1,000 year Kingdom reign.

––––––––––––––––––⟨◇◈◇⟩––––––––––––––––––

QUESTION H – How can a person be assured of taking part in the Rapture?

ANSWER:
First of all, the individual needs to be 100% certain they are indeed born-again. Being born-again means to have come to the cross of Jesus Christ in all humility and acknowledging Him as their Saviour. Please see the Special Invitation at the end of this book if you would like to be "born-again".

Once a person is born-again, they should begin to show evidence of this experience. They will have a desire to read God's word and pray to the Lord. In this new life as a Christian, the person will seek to be led by the Holy Spirit in obedience to God's word.

The Word of God indicates that only those who have "*kept GOD'S word*" and who have "*not defiled their garments*" are counted worthy of escaping the Tribulation period. Some born-again believers are given the chance of escape because they heeded the Word of God and did what it says. They separated themselves from this world and pleased God by their righteous walk with Him as King.

To be assured of taking part in the Rapture of First Fruit believers, the person should continue living a sanctified life that will be pleasing to Him. They should make every effort to be found blameless in the Lord's eyes. Finally, they should:

> *WATCH ye therefore, and PRAY ALWAYS, that ye may be accounted worthy to escape all these things that shall come to pass, and to stand before the Son of man.*
> (Luke 21:36(KJ)

QUESTION I – How can a Christian be excluded from the Kingdom? Aren't all Christians assured of going to Heaven?

ANSWER:
The distinction needs to be made between Heaven and the Kingdom of heaven. All born-again believers are assured of going to Heaven. Also, all overcomers enter the Kingdom because their names are written in the Lamb's book of life:

> *But there shall by no means enter it anything that defiles, or causes an abomination or a lie, but **only those who are written in the Lamb's Book of Life.***
> (Revelation 21:27 – NKJV)

Only those whose names have not been written in the Lamb's book of life will miss heaven:

If anyone's name was not found written in the book of life, he was thrown into the lake of fire. (Rev. 20:15)

Entrance into the Kingdom is another matter. The Kingdom refers to the 1,000 year reign with Christ known as the Millennium. Not all born-again believers are assured of taking part in this Kingdom:

*Not everyone who says to me, Lord, Lord, will enter the **Kingdom of heaven**, but only he who does the will of my Father who is in heaven.* (Matthew 7:21)

These are our Lord's own words that not all Christians will enter the Kingdom of heaven, or the 1,000 year reign with Him. In addition to other parables referred to in Matthew 7, the Lord also taught this concept in Luke 20:35:

*But those who are considered **worthy** of taking part in **that age** and in the resurrection from the dead...*

Jesus said only those who are considered worthy will take part in **that age** or the Kingdom age.

At the end of the Millennium, all Christians who missed the Kingdom reign will be raised to life. Since their names are written in the book of life, they are assured of going to Heaven at that time. While all Christians will not participate in the 1,000 year Kingdom reign, all true Christians will go to Heaven.

––––––––––––––––––––⋞◈⋟––––––––––––––––––––

QUESTION J – Why hasn't the Church been taught about the phased Rapture and the concept of the Kingdom?

ANSWER:
Remember, Ecclesiastes 3:15 tells us everything that is, has been before: "Whatever is has already been, and what will be has been before..."

When Jesus observed the condition of the church and its leaders notice what He had to say in Matthew 23:13-14:

> *Woe to you, teachers of the law and Pharisees, you hypocrites! You shut the kingdom of heaven in men's faces. You yourselves do not enter, nor will you let those enter who are trying to.*

Nothing has really changed from the time of Jesus. The religious leaders at that time were not teaching what the people needed to know. They were really hypocrites keeping others from the correct path.

Today, the same thing is happening again. Teachings about a partial or phased Rapture and the Kingdom are not being taught because it is the truth. The current day Pastors and teachers are, once again, keeping the people from entering the Kingdom, by not "rightly dividing" the word of truth.

Instead, much of the church is guilty of allowing incorrect teachings to prevail. No longer is sound doctrine encouraged as it should be (Titus 1:9 & 2:1), but the church has fulfilled yet another Scripture:

> *For the time will come when men will not put up with sound doctrine. Instead, to suit their own desires, they will gather around them a great number of teachers to say what their itchy ears want to hear..* (II Tim. 4:3)

The religious leaders of today need to re-evaluate what is being taught. The church members need to insist upon the return to sound doctrine.

QUESTION K – What does it mean to be an overcomer?

ANSWER:
An overcomer is a believer who has had an authentic experience with God. Though thrown into the furnace of affliction, they have come forth as pure gold. The overcomer is born through the victory they receive by trusting in Jesus Christ.

Learning to be an overcomer is perhaps the most difficult thing to do on this earth as a human being. Possessing impressive credentials and degrees offer little solace when it comes to where the "rubber meets the road." Every professing Christian must learn to be an overcomer through faith and total trust in their Savior.

In Matthew 11:28-30(KJ), Jesus urges:

> *Come unto me, all ye that labour and are heavy laden, and I will give you rest. Take my yoke upon you, and learn of me; for I am meek and lowly in heart: and ye shall find rest unto your souls. For my yoke is easy, and my burden is light.*

The overcomers take their agony and burdens to the mighty counselor. Through prayer and trust, Jesus leads the downcast believer to "green pasture." The sting of the adversary is somehow turned to sweet victory. Christ alone is able to provide the peace that passes all understanding.

While every believer will have trials and testing in this world, Christ reminded us to be of good cheer because He overcame this world. As believers, we find our sweet victory in Him! He has already overcome for us. Overcomers are believers who find their strength and help in Him--not through man, but by the power of the Son of God.

A genuine overcomer follows in Christ's footsteps. They learn to "take it on the chin" and to "take it to the cross." Whatever the world dishes out is handled with prayer and placed on the altar before God. By offering everything to Christ, they find hope and sufficiency in Him.

Being an overcomer is what being a Christian is all about. Through the trials of this life, the overcomer's faith is put on trial and thereby confirmed as Holy evidence before a mighty God, it is authentic.

As our example, Jesus endured the cross for the joy set before him. Overcomers have the victory because of His victory. Through His victory, the overcomer is able to walk in newness of life. The overcomer knows they have been crucified with Christ their old life is gone (Gal.2:20). By dying to self, the overcomer experiences the joy of Christ's triumph in their life.

Finally, an overcomer is grateful and humble, for they know of God's rich mercy and marvelous grace. If it wasn't for Christ, they would be doomed. Out of this gratitude, rises the song of gladness and praise. An overcomers' heart bursts forth with praise and adoration unto their God for the victory He provides.

The overcomer knows, first hand, that while weeping may endure for the night, joy cometh in the morning!

QUESTION L – What did Jesus mean by, *"Occupy until I come?"* (Luke 19:13)

ANSWER:
In the parable of the pounds, Jesus was teaching that His faithful followers should be diligent until He returns.

In the past, when people thought the Lord was about to return, they quit their jobs and sold their possessions. Unless the Lord told the individual to do this, this type of behavior is contrary to what the above verse teaches.

The believer should be diligently doing whatever they have been called to do. At the same time, however, some take the above verse as an excuse for not looking for Christ's return.

This extreme is not correct either. The believer should be diligent; but, at the same time, should also be looking for the Lord to return.

Looking for Him is an attitude of the person's heart. While we should continue living our lives doing what the Lord has called us to do, we should also understand that this world is not our home. The believer's true home is in Heaven, and we are really strangers just passing through this world (please see I Peter 2:11 and I John 2:15).

The believer needs to learn to balance diligently working at those things they have been called to do, along with looking for and eagerly awaiting His soon return.

QUESTION M – Why is the Blessed Hope important to the Believer?

ANSWER:
The Blessed Hope is so very important to the believer for several reasons.

First of all, looking for the Blessed Hope of the Lord's soon return is sound doctrine. The reader is encouraged to read the first and second chapters of Titus where Paul tells the importance of sound doctrine.

Sound doctrine should be encouraged and taught. Any who refute sound doctrine should be rebuked and encouraged back to sound doctrine.

"Looking for that Blessed Hope..." is sound doctrine that needs to be taught to all believers.

Second of all, having the Blessed Hope, the believers will purify themselves:

> *Everyone who has this hope in him purifies himself, just as he is pure.* (I John 3:3)

Knowing that the Lord will return very soon, the believers know that they will stand before a Holy God at that time. Having this hope in their heart, the believers are motivated to live a holy and blameless life. They will want to purify their hearts, knowing they will be with Him very soon. Finally, as was noted in II Timothy 4:8, one of the crowns that can be obtained is the **crown of righteousness** for those who **love His appearing**.

Those who love His appearing will be given this special crown. Having the Blessed Hope in ones heart should motivate the believer to long for and truly love the thought of being with Him. This will result in the believer receiving a glorious crown.

The Blessed Hope is a very important hope that every believer should have.

QUESTION N – Haven't you forgotten that we are saved by Grace?

ANSWER:
God's Grace is provided for believers to be overcomers. His Grace is not divine favor extended to the believer for continuance in any form of unholy behavior.

His Grace enables committed believers, empowered by His Spirit, through genuine repentance, to be overcomers. By God's Grace, through faith in Christ, the believer is able to break the chains of darkness and live a victorious life in Him.

Christ, alone, is able to heal and make whole. His beautiful gift of Grace is sufficient. Being justified by His Grace, we have the hope of eternal life:

> ...*having been justified by His grace, we might become heirs having the hope of eternal life. This is a trustworthy saying. And I want you to stress these things, so that those who have trusted in God may be careful to devote themselves to doing what is good.* (Titus 3:7&8)

This position of Grace is sacred, and should be deeply respected.

Too many people have misunderstood God's Grace. Often His Grace is perceived as a level of assurance which enables them to go along in their same uncommitted behavior. Erroneously, they believe God's Grace will counteract their uncommitted and un-yielded life. They have assumed Grace means erase with no consequences for their actions.

While we are saved by Grace, our salvation does not assure us that we will be found worthy to escape the Tribulation period. While salvation is completely free, escape from the Tribulation and entrance into the Kingdom will be based upon how the believer has utilized that free gift.

Peter tells us in II Peter 3:18: "...***grow*** *in the grace and knowledge of our Lord and Savior Jesus Christ...*" Peter is reminding the believer to continue to grow in God's grace. To grow in His grace means to "*make every effort to be found spotless, blameless and at peace with Him*" (please see II Peter

3:10-18).Through the sanctifying work of the Spirit, the believer will grow in the Grace of God.

The overcoming First Fruit believer realizes that he has to give over areas of his own life to be triumphant by His marvelous Grace. This is completely different from the "lukewarm" view which says that God's Grace will look over those areas because of His Grace. Grace then becomes a bandage to cover an unclean life. As Jude 4, says:

> *For certain men whose condemnation was written about long ago have secretly slipped in among you. They are godless men, who change the GRACE of God into a license for immorality.*

We are justified freely by God's marvelous Grace (Romans 3:24). That Grace, however, should not be used as a license to sin. God will not be mocked.

Jesus is our answer, not our excuse.

––––––––––––––––––––––––––◇◆◇––––––––––––––––––––––––––

QUESTION O – What does it mean to be "watching?"

ANSWER:

> *So Christ was once offered to bear the sins of many; **and unto them that look for him shall he appear the second time** without sin unto salvation.* (Hebrews 9:28)

The Word of God says that Jesus is returning the second time to those who are looking for him to return. Are you looking for Jesus to come again? If not, now is the time to start your watch because it is much later than most people think.

We do not know for certain the exact time that Jesus will return. Just before Jesus left this earth the first time he told His disciples that He was going to return and He commanded them to "Watch." What does it mean to continue watching?

Watching is an attitude of the heart that is truly looking for the soon return of the Lord. It was commanded by the Lord and some of the things *"Watching"* entails include:

1) Being aware of the prophetic signs in God's word.
2) Living a life of Holiness before our Lord.
3) Living a life separated from the world.
4) Encouraging one another with the wonderful Hope of His soon return.
5) Telling others Jesus is coming soon and that they need to be ready.
6) Praying the prayer Jesus taught us to pray in Luke 21:

> *And take heed to yourselves, lest at any time your hearts be overcharged with surfeiting, and drunkenness, and cares of this life, and so that day come upon you unawares. For as a snare shall it come on all them that dwell on the face of the whole earth.* **Watch ye, therefore, and pray always, that ye may be accounted worthy to escape all these things that shall come to pass, and to stand before the Son of man**
> (Luke 21:34-36).

The words from Matthew Henry's commentary are also very good advice for the wise:

> "Therefore every day and every hour we must be ready, and not off our watch any day in the year, or any hour in the day." (M. H. Volume 5, Page 372)

A poem about the virgins in Matthew 25:1-13

THE BRIDE

A lamp with oil
All 10 did possess
But, remember, 5 were wise
And 5 were foolish.
Those who were wise
Heeded the call
By hearing God's voice:
"Give me your all"
The foolish however
Squandered their worth
They did not shine for Jesus
Nor the people on earth.
They heard "The Cry"
Along with the wise
This is how the foolish
Were taken by surprise:
Their light became impoverished
For their joy did not spread
The 'oil of gladness' for them
Flickered out instead.
But the wise grew brighter
With a special over-flow
The more they loved Jesus
They gained a purer glow.
Though the cry was mighty
Five questioned the call
They could not comprehend:
'Come give me your all.'
For if they truly loved Him
They would have understood the plea
For hidden in the message is:
'My Beloved come to Me.'
The 5 wise virgins heard this impassioned cry
....And answered 'Yes, my Beloved,
I am coming, it is I'
So they laid it all down
Living only to serve
The moral of the 10 virgins is:
Each got what they deserve.

Appendix B – Glossary

ARMAGEDDON

That great battle at the end of the Tribulation period when Jesus Christ returns with His Saints to defeat the Antichrist and his armies. (Revelation 16:16)

BLESSED HOPE

The glorious promise that Jesus Christ will return for His own prior to the Tribulation period. (Titus 2:13)

BRIDE

Those born-again believers who have prepared themselves to meet the Lord. (Revelation 19:7-9) (Also see First Fruit believer and Overcomer.)

BRIDEGROOM

Jesus Christ (Revelation 19:9, and Matthew 25:5)

DAY OF THE LORD

Period of time that begins with the Tribulation period. Also includes the 1,000 year period also known as the Millennium. (I Thessalonians 5:2 & 4)

FIRST COMING

Christ's first arrival on the scene at His birth which probably took place on September 11, 3 BC.

FIRST FRUIT BELIEVER

Born-again believer found worthy by the Lord to be Raptured prior to the Tribulation period. Also referred to as Overcomer or bride of Christ. Called the Male Child in Revelation 12:5 (Rev. 14:4, Rev. 2:26-27, and Rev. 3:10).

HARVEST

Gathering of all who remain at the end of the Tribulation period (see Rev. 14:14-20, Luke 3: 17 and Matthew 13:30).

KINGDOM

The 1,000 year reign with Jesus Christ as the King of Kings. Also known as the Millennium (Rev 20:5-6 and Luke 20:35).

MALE CHILD

The First Fruit believer or the Saint known as an Overcomer. Taken up to the Throne of God prior to the Tribulation since he is considered worthy to escape (Rev. 12:5, Rev. 14:4, and Rev. 2:26-27).

MILLENNIUM

The 1,000 year reign with Jesus Christ as King. Also known as the Kingdom, or the 7th day or the last 1,000 years of God's 7 years of man (Rev. 20:4).

NOMINAL CHRISTIAN

A person who calls himself a Christian, but in reality is not truly born-again. Also known as a professing Christian (II Tim. 3:5 and I John 2:4-6).

OVERCOMER

Born-again believer who has died to self and lives to please God by a holy, righteous and blameless walk. One who has kept the Word of God and is looking for the soon return of the Lord. Also see First Fruit believer, Male Child and the bride (please see chapter 5).

PENTECOST

Feast that falls on the 6th of Sivan. Known as the Feast of Weeks, the Feast of Harvest and the day of Firstfruits. The day that Enoch was born and Raptured. Church began at Pentecost, and it is very possible that the Rapture of the First Fruit believers could take place on this Feast (Exodus 23:14-16; Exodus 34:22 and Numbers 28:26).

PROPHETIC YEAR

Length of year as sometimes measured by God: 360 days. See Genesis 7:11 and 8:3. (As opposed to a Solar year which is 365.25 days long.)

RAPTURE

Removal of born-again believers from the earth. Enoch being a type-picture for the First Fruit believers (Genesis 5:24). The Rapture of First Fruit believers is found in Revelation 12:5 and in Rev. 14:1-5. Also referred to in II Thessalonians 2:7).

SECOND COMING

The return of the Lord at the end of the Tribulation period and at the end of the 6,000 years of man (Rev. 14:14-20, Rev. 20:11-21 and Matthew 24:30-31). Saints return with the Lord at this time as shown in Jude 14, to judge everyone and to rule with an iron scepter (Rev. 2:27).

TRIBULATION

Period of time that begins right after the Rapture of First Fruit believers and then followed by the appearance of the Antichrist. Ends with the return of the Lord at the Second Coming with His saints to fight the battle of Armageddon.

UPWARD CALLING

High calling referred to by the Apostle Paul in Philippians 3:14. For those Saints alive when the Tribulation is about to begin, it also refers to escaping that time. It also is referring to being able to reign with the Lord during the Millennial Kingdom.

The end of the age is coming soon. Therefore be earnest, thoughtful men of prayer.
(I Peter 4:7 – Paraphrase)

Appendix C – Overcomers' Prayer

Jesus teaches His disciples in Matthew 6:9-15, how we should pray, by giving us what is known as: "the Lord's Prayer."

"9) In this manner, therefore, pray:

Our Father in heaven,
Jesus tells us to pray to our Father in heaven which should give us confidence to know who we are praying to.

Hallowed be Your name.
We are to acknowledge Him with deep reverence for who He is.

10) Your kingdom come.
Until Jesus returns, we are to pray for His coming Kingdom. The entire Sermon on the Mount is devoted to instructing the overcomer on how they are to live their new life as His disciple in order to qualify to enter into His coming Kingdom. Jesus lists this here as one of the top priorities they should pray for.

Your will be done On earth as it is in heaven.
Next, Jesus tells us we should submit our will on this earth to God's will in heaven. God has a perfect will (Rom. 12:2) for each of His people and He wants us to submit our life to Him.

11) Give us this day our daily bread.
After recognizing God's name, God's coming Kingdom, and then God's will, Jesus then instructs us to pray for our needs in complete dependence upon Him.

Notice we are to pray only for our <u>daily</u> bread (physical food and spiritual food) for each new day. He wants us to live by faith knowing that He will supply our needs and that we do not need to worry about tomorrow's bread.

12) *And forgive us our debts,*

The next thing we should ask our heavenly Father for is forgiveness of any and all failings on our part. This would include our sins, trespasses and failures against Him or others.

As we forgive our debtors.

This is an acknowledgement that we are to forgive other people when they commit trespasses against us. Jesus goes into this subject later on (verses 14 and 15 below) after He completes the main points of this model prayer.

13) *And do not lead us into temptation,*

Jesus then tells us to pray that God will not lead us into temptation. The Greek word for temptation is # 3986 (peirasmos) which can represent a trial or test that can be sent by God and serve to test or prove one's character or faith.

It is extremely important to note that this is the exact same term that Jesus uses in His promise to the Church of Philadelphia:

> *"Since you have kept my command ("word – KJ) to endure patiently,* **I will also keep you from the hour of trial** *that is going to come upon the whole world to test those who live on the earth."* (Revelation 3:10 – NIV)

The Church of Philadelphia is the one faithful Church who keeps God's word and is given the wonderful promise of being kept from the *"hour of trial"* which represents the Tribulation period.

In other words, in the Lord's prayer, Jesus is telling the overcomer that they should be praying for God to deliver them from the coming Tribulation period. This is the promise given to the Church of Philadelphia and it is also the same prayer Jesus later instructs His disciples to pray when telling them about the day that is coming unexpectedly as a snare:

*"34) But take heed to yourselves, lest your hearts be weighed down with carousing, drunkenness, and cares of this life, and **that Day come on you unexpectedly.** 35) For **it will come as a snare** on all those who dwell on the face of the whole earth. 36) **Watch therefore, and pray always that you may be counted worthy to escape all these things** that will come to pass, and to stand before the Son of Man.* (Luke 21: 34-36 – NKJV)

This confirms that there is an escape from the Tribulation period for those who are **praying** that they may be counted worthy to escape it. The overcomer will be regularly praying for God to count them worthy to be kept from the coming Tribulation period.

But deliver us from the evil one.
The very next part of the verse confirms that we are to pray for God to deliver us from the coming Antichrist who will be the ruler on the earth during the Tribulation period.

Most of the modern day Church has no idea that the Lord's prayer instructs us to pray for deliverance from the coming Tribulation period. This is one of the reasons that this appendix was called the *"Overcomers' Prayer."* The overcomer has ears to hear these instructions given to them by the Lord and they are actively praying this prayer for deliverance from the coming Tribulation period on a regular basis.

For Yours is the kingdom and the power and the glory forever. Amen.
Jesus then ends this model prayer by affirming that the Kingdom, Power and Glory all belong to God both now and forever more.

Jesus then footnotes His prayer by reminding us:
14) For if you forgive men their trespasses, your heavenly Father will also forgive you.

15) But if you do not forgive men their trespasses, neither will your Father forgive your trespasses."
(Matthew 6:9-15 – NKJV)

These concluding remarks by Jesus make it clear that it is important for us to forgive others when they commit trespasses against us. This is an important warning that the overcomer will take very seriously to ensure that they do not hold or nurse any grudges when wronged by others.

Partial or Phased Rapture

It is important to point out that our Lord alludes to the doctrine of a "partial" or "phased" Rapture of believers in both the earlier and later portions of His ministry. First, in the Sermon on the Mount, Jesus teaches His disciples to pray for deliverance from the Tribulation period (v.13). Towards the very end of His ministry when He gives His famous discourse on the Mount of Olives He also instructs His followers to always pray for escape from the same Tribulation period (Luke 21:34-36 above).

Jesus chose to teach His disciples this principle of a "partial" or "phased" Rapture on two different occasions. Both times were on a "Mount," both times He taught this privately to His disciples, and both times He included this important instruction in a prayer for His disciples to follow. The overcomer has the ears to hear and the heart to understand this teaching while the rest of the Church prefers to follow the Traditions of man (Colossians 2:8).

The overcomer heeds the Lord's advice and prays for deliverance from the coming Tribulation period on a continual basis.

Appendix D – Signs of Christ's Coming

———————◇◆◇———————

Many modern Bible teachers and students believe that the rebirth of the nation of Israel represents the budding of the *fig tree* that Jesus described to His disciples as he sat on the Mount of Olives, and we are living in the generation that won't pass away before He returns.

Verily I say unto you, this generation shall not pass, till all these things be fulfilled. (Matthew 24:34 – KJV)

With Israel becoming a nation in 1948, we have been alerted that the Lord's return is fast approaching. Jesus also told his disciples a second sign to look for in the parable of Noah:

As it was in the days of Noah, so it will be at the coming of the Son of Man.
(Matthew 24:37 – NIV)

Here the Lord is telling the Church that just prior to His return, things will be the same as they were back in Noah's day. This pictures life going on right up until the day that the rapture occurs, and the judgments of God are suddenly released upon the earth. A careful study of Genesis 6 will alert the reader to the fact that living in these end times is almost parallel to the time before the flood. The world has become a great cesspool of corruption, violence, sex, drugs, idolatry, witchcraft and other perversions. Reading the account in Genesis is like reading today's newspaper or listening to the daily news.

In the Lord's parable concerning Noah, Jesus was also giving us a second important sign that His return is drawing very near. Several years ago a famous comet passed though our solar system and it was hailed at the most watched comet of all times.

Sign of Christ's Coming

———————⟨◇⟩———————

April 8, 1997

Comet Hale-Bopp Over New York City
Credit and Copyright: J. Sivo
http://antwrp.gsfc.nasa.gov/apod/ap970408.html
"What's that point of light above the World Trade Center? It's
Comet Hale-Bopp! Both faster than a speeding bullet and able
to "leap" tall buildings in its single <u>orbit</u>, Comet Hale-Bopp is
also bright enough to be seen even over the glowing lights of
one of the world's premier cities. In the foreground lies the East
River, while much of New York City's Lower Manhattan can
be seen between the river and the comet."

———————⟨◇⟩———————

**As it was in the days of Noah, so it will be at the coming of
the Son of Man.** (Matthew 24:37 – NIV)

These words from our wonderful Lord have several applications about the Tribulation period that is about to ensnare this world.

Seas Lifted Up

Throughout the Old Testament, the time of the coming Tribulation period is described as the time when the "seas have lifted up," and also as coming in as a "flood" (please see Jeremiah 51:42, Hosea 5:10, Daniel 11:40 and Psalm 93:3-4 for just a few examples).

This is a direct parallel to the time of Noah when the Great Flood of water came to wipe out every living creature except for righteous Noah and his family, and the pairs of animals God spared. While God said He would never flood the earth again with water, the coming Judgement will be by fire (II Peter 3:10). The book of Revelation shows that approximately three billion people will perish in the terrible time that lies ahead (see Revelation 6:8 and 9:15).

2 Witnesses

A guiding principle of God is to establish a matter based upon the witness of two or more:

> ...*a matter must be established by the testimony of two or three witnesses* (Deuteronomy 19:15 – NIV)

In 1994, God was able to get the attention of mankind when Comet Shoemaker-Levy crashed into Jupiter on the 9th of Av (on the Jewish calendar). Interestingly, this Comet was named after the "two" witnesses who first discovered it.

In 1995, "two" more astronomers also discovered another comet. It was called Comet Hale-Bopp, and it reached its closest approach to planet Earth on March 23, 1997. It has been labeled as the most widely viewed comet in the history of mankind.

Scientists have determined that Comet Hale-Bopp's orbit brought it to our solar system 4,465 years ago (see Notes 1 and 2 below). In other words, the comet made its appearance near Earth in 1997 and also in 2468 BC. Remarkably, this comet preceded the Great Flood by 120 years! God warned Noah of this in Genesis 6:3:

> *My Spirit shall not strive with man forever, for he is indeed flesh; yet his days shall be one hundred and twenty years.*

Days of Noah
What does all of this have to do with the Lord's return? Noah was born around 2948 BC, and Genesis 7:11, tells us that the Flood took place when Noah was 600, or in 2348 BC.

Remember, our Lord told us: *"As it was in the days of Noah, so it will be at the coming of the Son of Man.* (Matthew 24:37 – NIV)

In the original Greek, it is saying: *"exactly like"* it was, so it will be when He comes (see Strong's #5618).

During the days of Noah, Comet Hale-Bopp arrived on the scene as a harbinger of the Great Flood. Just as this same comet appeared before the Flood, could its arrival again in 1997 be a sign that God's final Judgement, also known as the time of Jacob's Trouble, is about to begin?

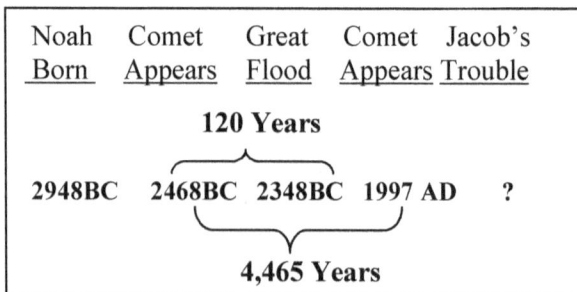

Noah Born	Comet Appears	Great Flood	Comet Appears	Jacob's Trouble
		120 Years		
2948BC	2468BC	2348BC	1997 AD	?
		4,465 Years		

Comet Hale-Bopp's arrived 120 years before the Flood as a warning to mankind. Only righteous Noah heeded God's warning and built the ark, as God instructed. By faith, Noah was obedient to God and, as a result, saved himself and his family from destruction.

Remember, Jesus told us His return would be preceded by great heavenly signs: *"And there shall be signs in the sun, and in the moon, and in the stars; and upon the earth distress of nations, with perplexity; the sea and the waves roaring..."* (Luke 21:25)

Just as this large comet appeared as a 120-year warning to Noah, its arrival in 1997 tells us that Jesus is getting ready to return again. Is this the **"Sign"** Jesus referred to?

Jesus was asked 3 questions by the disciples:
*"Tell us, (1) when shall these things be" (the destruction of the city of Jerusalem, " and (2) what shall be the **sign** of thy coming, and (3) of the end of the world?"* (Matthew 24:3)

Sign of Christ's Coming

The **first** question had to do with events that were fulfilled in 70 AD. The **third** question has to do with the future time at the very end of the age.

The **second** question, however, has to do with the time of Christ's second coming. Jesus answered this second question in His description of the days of Noah found in Matthew 24:33-39:

*[33] So likewise ye, when ye shall see all these things, know that it is near, even at the doors. [34] Verily I say unto you, This generation shall not pass, till all these things be fulfilled. [35] Heaven and earth shall pass away, but my words shall not pass away. [36] But of that day and hour knoweth no man, no, not the angels of heaven, but my Father only. [37] **But as the days of Noe were, so shall also the coming of the Son***

of man be. *(38)For as in the days that were before the flood they were eating and drinking, marrying and giving in marriage, until the day that Noe entered into the ark, (39) And knew not until the flood came, and took them all away; so shall also the coming of the Son of man be.*

Jesus is telling us that the **_sign_** of His coming will be as it was during the days of Noah. As Comet Hale-Bopp was a sign to the people in Noah's day, its arrival in 1997 is a sign that Jesus is coming back again soon. Comet Hale-Bopp could be the very sign Jesus was referring to, which would announce His return for His faithful.

Remember, Jesus said, *"exactly as it was in the days of Noah, so will it be when He returns."* The appearance of Comet Hale-Bopp in 1997 is a strong indication that the Tribulation period is about to begin, but before then, Jesus is coming for His bride!

Keep looking up! Jesus is coming again very soon!
As Noah prepared for the destruction God warned him about 120 years before the Flood, Jesus has given mankind a final warning that the Tribulation period is about to begin. The horrible destruction on 9/11 is only a precursor of what is about to take place on planet Earth. We need to be wise like Noah and prepare. Always remember our Lord's instructions:

Watch and Pray

(34)And take heed to yourselves, lest at any time your hearts be overcharged with surfeiting, and drunkenness, and cares of this life, and so that day come upon you unawares. (35) For as a snare shall it come on all them that dwell on the face of the whole earth.(36)Watch ye therefore, and pray always, that ye may be accounted worthy to escape all these things that shall come to pass, and to stand before the Son of man (Luke 21:34-36).

Footnotes to Appendix D

(1) The original orbit of Comet Hale-Bopp was calculated to be approximately 265 years by engineer George Sanctuary in his article, ***Three Craters In Israel***, published on 3/31/01 found in the Supplemental Articles at www.ProphecyCountdown.com

Comet Hale-Bopp's orbit around the time of the Flood changed from 265 years to about 4,200 years. Because the plane of the comet's orbit is perpendicular to the earth's orbital plane (ecliptic), Mr. Sanctuary noted: "A negative time increment was used for this simulation...to back the comet away from the earth.... past Jupiter... and then out of the solar system. The simulation suggests that the past-past orbit had a very eccentric orbit with a period of only 265 years. When the comet passed Jupiter (***around 2203BC***) its orbit was deflected upward, coming down near the earth 15 months later with the comet's period changed from 265 years to about (***4,200***) years." (***added text for clarity***)

(2) Don Yeomans, with NASA's Jet Propulsion Laboratory, made the following observations regarding the comet's orbit: "By integrating the above orbit forward and backward in time until the comet leaves the planetary system and then referring the osculating orbital elements...the following orbital periods result: Original orbital period before entering planetary system = 4200 years. Future orbital period after exiting the planetary system = 2380 years."

This analysis can be found at:

http://www2.jpl.nasa.gov/comet/ephcmjpl6.html

Based upon the above two calculations we have the following:

265 [a] + 4,200 [b] = 4,465 Years

1997 AD – 4,465 Years = 2468 BC = Hale Bopp arrived

(a) Orbit period calculated by George Sanctuary before deflection around 2203 BC.

(b) Orbit period calculated by Don Yeomans after 1997 visit.

Tract Included In Appendix D

This tract was written in 1997 when Comet Hale-Bopp entered our solar system. In 2027 it will be the 30th Anniversary of its last appearance. Bullinger wrote, "30, being 3x10 denotes in a higher degree the perfection of Divine order, as marking the **right moment**. Christ was thirty years of age at the commencement of His ministry. David was also 30 when he began to reign." (Bullinger, p. 265). Was Comet Hale-Bopp giving us a sign that the bride of Christ is about to begin her reign very soon? NOT setting a date, just sounding the alarm (please see Ezekiel 33:2-6).

A Final Reminder

Upon finishing this book, the reader should realize that the process of being an overcomer is not an easy assignment that can be accomplished within our own power. The world, our flesh and the devil will attempt to defeat us every single day.

In order to be successful overcomers we must continually die to self (Matthew 16:24) and allow the Holy Spirit to direct and empower our lives. This involves a daily victory along a narrow path (Matthew 7:13-14) that few desire to follow.

Realizing that none of us can be successful in our own strength, we must learn to place our life in Christ's loving hands:

> *I am the vine, you are the branches. He who abides in Me, and I in him, bears much fruit; for without Me you can do nothing.* (John 15:5 – NKJV)

Only by abiding in Jesus and being filled with the Holy Spirit can we exhibit the fruit of His life to this fallen world.

May the reader be encouraged that Jesus will help you be the overcomer He wants you to be as we come unto Him:

> *Come to Me, all you who labor and are heavy laden, and I will give you rest. Take My yoke upon you and learn from Me, for I am gentle and lowly in heart, and you will find rest for your souls. For My yoke is easy and My burden is light.*
> (Matthew 11:28-30 – NKJV)

Special Invitation

This book was primarily written to those who have been born again. If you have never been born again, would you like to be? The Bible shows that it's simple to be saved...

- **Realize you are a sinner.**
  "As it is written, There is none righteous, no, not one:" (Romans 3:10)
  "... for there is no difference. For all have sinned, and come short of the glory of God;" (Romans 3:22-23)

- **Realize you CAN NOT save yourself.**
  "But we are all as an unclean thing, and all our righteousness are as filthy rags; ..." (Isaiah 64:6)
  "Not by works of righteousness which we have done, but according to his mercy he saved us, ..." (Titus 3:5)

- **Realize that Jesus Christ died on the cross to pay for your sins.**
  "Who his own self bare our sins in his own body on the tree, ..." (I Peter 2:24)
  "... Unto him that loved us, and washed us from our sins in his own blood," (Revelation 1:5)

- **Simply by faith receive Jesus Christ as your personal Savior.**
  "But as many as received him, to them gave he power to become the sons of God, even to them that believe on his name:" (John 1:12)
  " ...Sirs, what must I do to be saved? And they said, Believe on the Lord Jesus Christ, and thou shalt be saved, and thy house." (Acts 16:30-31)

WOULD YOU LIKE TO BE SAVED?

If you would like to be saved, believe on the Lord Jesus Christ right now by making this acknowledgment in your heart:

> Lord Jesus, I know that I am a sinner, and unless You save me, I am lost forever. I thank You for dying for me at Calvary. By faith I come to You now, Lord, the best way I know how, and ask You to save me. I believe that God raised You from the dead and acknowledge You as my personal Saviour.

If you believed on the Lord, this is the most important decision of your life. You are now saved by the precious blood of Jesus Christ, which was shed for you and your sins. Now that you have received Jesus as your personal Saviour, you will want to find a Church where you can be baptized as your first act of obedience, and where the Word of God is taught so you can continue to grow in your faith. Ask the Holy Spirit to help you as you read the Bible to learn all that God has for your life.

Also, please see the pages that follow for information on several books that will help you on your wonderful journey and help you prepare for the days ahead.

Endtimes

The Bible indicates that we are living in the final days and Jesus Christ is getting ready to return very soon. This book was written to help Christians prepare for what lies ahead. The Word of God indicates that the Tribulation Period is rapidly approaching and that the Antichrist is getting ready to emerge on the world scene.

Jesus promised His disciples that there is a way to escape the horrible time of testing and persecution that will soon devastate this planet. The whole purpose of this book is to help you get prepared so you will rule and reign with Jesus when He returns.

About The Author

Jim Harman has been a Christian for more than 43 years. He has diligently studied the Word of God with a particular emphasis on Prophecy. Jim has written several books and the most essential titles are available at www.ProphecyCountdown.com: *The Coming Spiritual Earthquake, The Kingdom, Overcomers' Guide To The Kingdom, Calling All Overcomers, Daniel's Prophecies Unsealed and Salvation of the Soul;* which have been widely distributed around the world. These books will encourage you to continue *"Looking"* for the Lord's soon return.

Jim's professional experience included being a Certified Public Accountant (CPA) and a Certified Property Manager (CPM). He had an extensive background in both public accounting and financial management with several well known national firms.

Jim has been fortunate to have been acquainted with several mature believers who understand and teach the deeper truths of the Bible. It is Jim's strong desire that many will come to realize the importance of seeking the Kingdom and seeking Christ's righteousness as we approach the soon return of our Lord and Saviour Jesus Christ.

The burden of his heart is to see many believers come to know the joy of Christ's triumph in their life as they become true overcomers; qualified and ready to rule and reign with Christ in the coming Kingdom.

To contact the author for questions or to arrange for speaking engagements:

Jim Harman
P.O. Box 941612
Maitland, FL 32794
JimHarmanCPA@aol.com

-125-

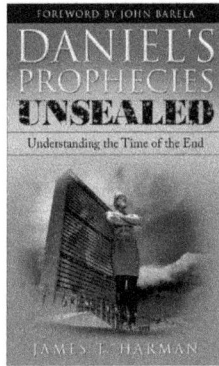

FOREWORD BY JOHN BARELA

DANIEL'S PROPHECIES

UNSEALED

Understanding the Time of the End

JAMES F. HARMAN

"Go your way Daniel, because the words are closed up and sealed until the time of the end...none of the wicked will understand, but those who are wise will understand."
(Daniel 12:9-10)

The Archangel Michael told Daniel that the prophecies would be sealed until the time of the end. Discover how the prophecies in the book of Daniel are being unsealed in the events taking place today.

Since Daniel was told that the wise will understand the message and lead many to righteousness, while the wicked will not grasp its meaning and will continue in their wickedness, it is imperative for everyone living in these end times to diligently examine and attempt to comprehend the vital message Daniel has recorded for us. The wise will diligently search the word of the Lord and ask for wisdom in order to understand God's plan.

When Jesus came the first time, the wise men of the day were aware of His soon arrival and they were actively looking for Him. Today, those who are wise will be passionately sharing this message and helping others prepare. Those doing so will *"shine like the stars forever and ever."*

May the Lord grant us a heart of wisdom to understand the time we are living in so we can prepare for what lies ahead!

Download your FREE copy: www.ProphecyCountdown.com

Or from Amazon.com–Available in Paperback and/or Kindle Edition

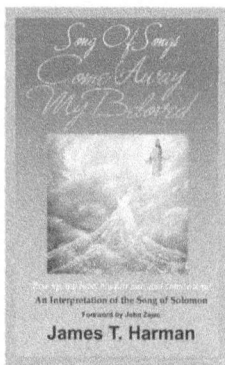

Song Of Songs
Come Away
My Beloved

An Interpretation of the Song of Solomon
Foreword by John Zajac
James T. Harman

God placed the Song of Solomon in the heart of the Bible for a special reason. *Come Away My Beloved* helps reveal that reason in a most enchanting way. In this refreshing commentary you will realize why this ancient love story has perplexed Bible students and commentators down through the ages.

Find out the prophetic importance veiled within the Song's poetic imagery and experience a renewed love for the Lord as you explore one of the most passionate love stories of all time.

Witness the wonderful joys of romance and devotion shared by two young lovers. Discover enduring lessons of virtue and faithfulness, and learn amazing truths that have been hidden within the greatest love Song ever written.

Written almost 3,000 years ago this brilliant Song of love reflects God's desire for every man and woman; not only in their present lives but also in their relationship with Him.

This book will revive your heart with a fervent love for your Saviour. It will also help you prepare for your glorious wedding day when Jesus returns for His devoted bride.

Allow this beautiful story of love and passion to ignite a flame in your heart and let this inspirational Song arouse your heart to join in the impassioned cry with the rest of the bride:

"Make haste, my beloved, and come quickly…"

Download your FREE copy: www.ProphecyCountdown.com

Or from Amazon.com–Available in Paperback and/or Kindle Edition

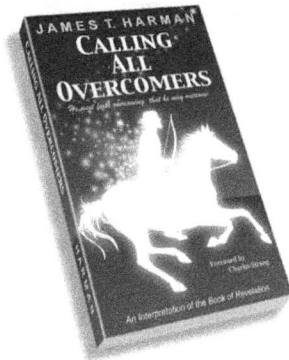

Perplexed by the book of Revelation? Not sure what all the signs, symbols and metaphors really mean? Jim Harman's latest work unravels Apostle John's remarkable revelation of Jesus Christ and what's in store for the inhabitants of planet Earth. This extraordinary commentary is not another cookie-cutter rehash of the popular teachings fostered by the *Left Behind* phenomena so prevalent in today's church.

One of the central messages in the book of Revelation is that God is calling men to be genuine overcomers. Jesus Christ has been sent out from the throne of God to conquer men's hearts so they can also be overcomers.

The purpose of this book is to encourage people to embrace Him as the King of their heart and allow His life to reign in theirs. He wants you to be able to overcome by His mighty power and strength living inside of you just as He overcame for all of us. Jesus will be looking for a faithful remnant qualified to rule and reign with Him when He returns. This book will help you prepare to be the overcomer for which Jesus is looking.

The reader will come away with a new and enlightened understanding of what the last book in God's Word is all about. Understand the book of Revelation and why it is so important for believers living in the last days of the Church age.

Download your FREE copy: www.ProphecyCountdown.com

Or from Amazon.com–Available in Paperback and/or Kindle Edition

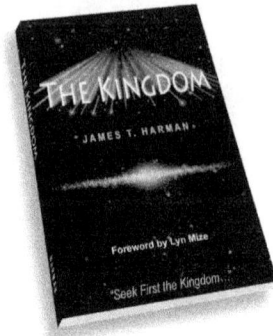

Once a person is saved, the number one priority should be seeking entrance into the Kingdom through the salvation of their soul. It is pictured as a runner in a race seeking a prize represented by a crown that will last forever.

The salvation of the soul and entrance into the coming Kingdom are only achieved through much testing and the trial of one's faith. If you are going through difficulty, then REJOICE:

> *"Blessed is the man who perseveres under trial, because when he has stood the test, he will receive the crown of life that God has promised to those who love Him."* (James 1:12)

The "Traditional" teaching on the "THE KINGDOM" has taken the Church captive into believing all Christians will rule and reign with Christ no matter if they have lived faithful and obedient lives, or if they have been slothful and disobedient with the talents God has given them. Find out the important Truth before Jesus Christ returns.

MUST READING FOR EVERY CHRISTIAN

Jesus Christ is returning for His faithful overcoming followers. Don't miss the opportunity of ruling and reigning with Christ in the coming KINGDOM!

Download your FREE copy: www.ProphecyCountdown.com

Or from Amazon.com – Available in Paperback and or Kindle Edition

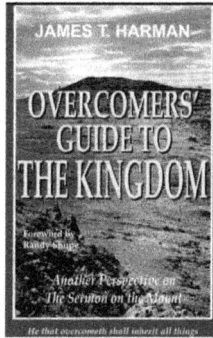

Get ready to climb back up the Mountain to listen to Christ's teachings once again. Though you may have read this great Sermon many times, discover exciting promises that many have missed.

The purpose of this book is to help Christians be the Overcomers Jesus wants them to be and to help them gain their own entrance in the coming Kingdom. Learn what seeking the Kingdom of God is all about and be among the chosen few who will "enter into" the coming Kingdom. *"Whoever hears these sayings of Mine, and does them, I will liken him to a wise man who built his house upon the rock."* (Matthew 7:24)

Also learn about:
- The link between Beatitudes and Fruit of the Spirit
- What the "law of Christ" really is
- The critical importance of the "Lord's prayer"
- How to be an Overcomer
- THE SIGN of Christ's soon Coming
- A new song entitled: LOOKING FOR THE SON which has the message of how vitally important it is to be Watching for the Lord's return and the consequences to those who are not looking.

Order your copy today from www.ProphecyCountdown.com

Or from Amazon.com – Available in Paperback and or Kindle Edition

LOOKING FOR THE SON
Lyrics by Jim Harman
Listen to this Song on the Home Page of Prophecy Countdown

Lyric	Scripture
There's a fire burning in my heart	Luke 24:32
Yearning for the Lord to come,	Rev. 22:17, Mat. 6:33
and His Kingdom come to start	
Soon He'll come.....so enter the narrow gate	Lk. 21:34-36,Mat.7:13
Even though you mock me now...	II Peter 3:4
He'll come to set things straight	
Watch how I'll leave in the twinkling of an eye	I Corinthians 15:52
Don't be surprised when I go up in the sky	Revelation 3:10
There's a fire burning in my heart	Luke 24:32
Yearning for my precious Lord	Revelation 22:17
And His Kingdom come to start	Revelation 20:4-6
Your love of this world, has forsaken His	I John 2:15
It leaves me knowing that you could have had it all	Revelation 21:7
Your love of this world, was oh so reckless	Revelation 3:14-22
I can't help thinking	Philippians 1:3-6
You would have had it all	Revelation 21:7
Looking for the Son	Titus 2:13, Luke 21:36
(Tears are gonna fall, not looking for the Son)	Matthew 25:10-13
You had His holy Word in your hand	II Timothy 3:16
(You're gonna wish you had listened to me)	Jeremiah 25:4-8
And you missed it...for your self	Matthew 22:11-14
(Tears are gonna fall, not looking for the Son)	Matthew 25:10-13
Brother, I have a story to be told	Habakkuk 2:2
It's the only one that's true	John 3:16-17
And it should've made your heart turn	II Peter 3:9
Remember me when I rise up in the air	I Corinthians 15:52
Leaving your home down here	I Corinthians 15:52
For true Treasures beyond compare	Matthew 6:20
Your love of this world, has forsaken His	I John 2:15
It leaves me knowing that you could have had it all	Revelation 21:7
Your love of this world, was oh so reckless	Revelation 3:14-22
I can't help thinking	Philippians 1:3-6
You would have had it all	Revelation 21:7

(Lyrics in parentheses represent background vocals)
(CONTINUED)

Lyric	Scripture
Looking for the Son	Titus 2:13, Lk. 21:36
(Tears are gonna fall, not looking for the Son)	Matthew 25:10-13
You had His holy Word in your hand	II Timothy 3:16
(You're gonna wish you had listened to me)	Jeremiah 25:4-8
And you lost it...for your self	Matthew 22:11-14
(Tears are gonna fall, not looking for the Son)	Matthew 25:10-13
You would have had it all	Revelation 21:7
Looking for the Son	Titus 2:13, Lk. 21:36
You had His holy Word in your hand	II Timothy 3:16
But you missed it... for your self	Matthew 22:11-14

Lov'n the world....not the open door — I Jn. 2:15, Rev. 4:1
Down the broad way... blind to what life's really for — Matthew 7:13-14
Turn around now...while there still is time — I Jn. 1:9, II Pet. 3:9
Learn your lesson now or you'll reap just what you sow — Galatians 6:7

(You're gonna wish you had listened to me)
You would have had it all
(Tears are gonna fall, not looking for the Son)
You would have had it all
(You're gonna wish you had listened to me)
It all, it all, it all
(Tears are gonna fall, not looking for the Son)

You would have had it all
(You're gonna wish you had listened to me)
Looking for the Son
(Tears are gonna fall, not looking for the Son)
You had His holy Word in your hand
(You're gonna wish you had listened to me)
And you missed it...for your self
(Tears are gonna fall, not looking for the Son)

You would have had it all
(You're gonna wish you had listened to me)
Looking for the Son
(Tears are gonna fall, not looking for the Son)
You had His holy Word in your hand
(You're gonna wish you had listened to me)
But you missed it
You missed it
You missed it
You missed it....for your self

Scripture Summary
Jeremiah 25:4-8
Habakkuk 2:2
Matthew 6:20
Matthew 6:33
Matthew 7:13
Matthew 22:11-14
Matthew 25:10-13
Luke 21:34-36
Luke 24:332
John 3:16-17
I Corinthians 15:52
Galatians 6:7
Philippians 1:3-6
II Timothy 3:16
Titus 2:13
II Peter 3:9
II Peter 3:4
I John 1:9
I John 2:15
Revelation 3:10
Revelation 3:14-22
Revelation 4:1
Revelation 20:4-6
Revelation 21:7
Revelation 22:17

(See www.ProphecyCountdown.com for more information)

The Day of the Lord is Near!

The Coming Spiritual Earthquake

by James T. Harman

"The Message presented in this book is greatly needed to awaken believers to the false ideas many have when it comes to the Rapture. I might have titled it: THE RAPTURE EARTH-QUAKE!"
Ray Brubaker - God's News Behind the News

"If I am wrong, anyone who follows the directions given in this book will be better off spiritually. If I am right, they will be among the few to escape the greatest spiritual calamity of the ages."
Jim Harman - Author

**MUST READING FOR EVERY CHRISTIAN!
HURRY! BEFORE IT IS TOO LATE!**